Table of Contents

Following Directions: What is a Game?

Directions: Read about games. Then, answer the questions.

A **game** is a contest or sport set by rules. Kayla likes to play games with her friends because it is fun, and she learns to play by the rules. Kayla and her friends also learn to be good winners and losers.

1. What is a **game**? ______________________________

2. What is your favorite game? ______________________________

3. Write the rules of this game. ______________________________

   a. ______________________________

   b. ______________________________

   c. ______________________________

   d. ______________________________

   e. ______________________________

Classifying: Outdoor/Indoor Games

Classifying is putting things that are alike into groups.

Directions: Read about games. Draw an **X** on the games you can play indoors. Circle the objects used for outdoor games.

Some games are outdoor games. Some games are indoor games. Outdoor games are active. Indoor games are quiet.

Which game do you like best? ______________________

Comprehension: Outdoor/Indoor Games

Directions: Read the story. Then, answer the questions.

Derrick likes to play outdoor and indoor games. His favorite outdoor game is baseball because he likes to hit the ball with the bat and run around the bases. He plays this game in the park with the neighborhood kids.

When it rains, he plays checkers with Lorenzo on the dining-room table in his apartment. He likes the game, because he has to use his brain to think about his next move, and the rules are easy to follow.

1. What is your favorite outdoor game? ______________________

____

2. Why do you like this game? ______________________

____

3. Where is this game played? ______________________

____

4. What is your favorite indoor game? ______________________

____

5. Why do you like this game? ______________________

____

6. Where is this game played? ______________________

____

Sequencing: 1, 2, 3, 4!

Directions: Write numbers by each sentence to show the order of the story.

__________ The pool is empty.

__________ Ben plays in the pool.

__________ Ben gets out.

__________ Ben fills the pool.

Comprehension: Types of Tops

The **main idea** is the most important point or idea in a story.

Directions: Read about tops. Then, answer the questions.

Tops come in all sizes. Some tops are made of wood. Some tops are made of tin. All tops do the same thing. They spin! Do you have a top?

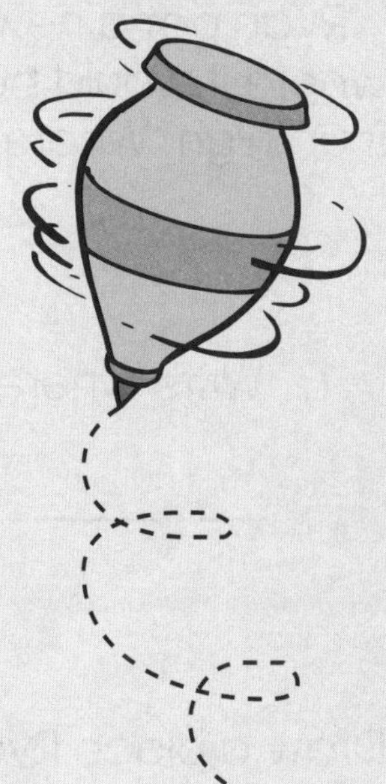

1. Circle the main idea:

   There are many kinds of tops.

   Some tops are made of wood.

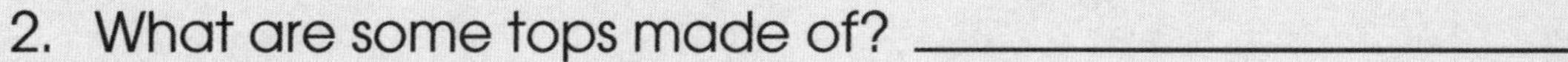

2. What are some tops made of? ____________________

3. What do all tops do? ____________________

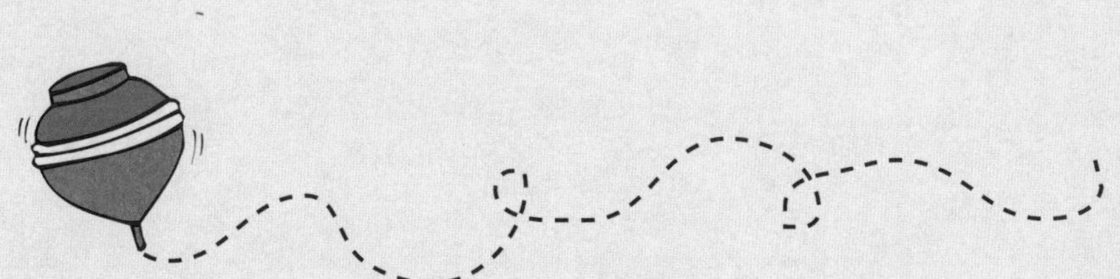

Making Inferences: Ryan's Top

Directions: Read about Ryan's top. Then, follow the instructions.

Ryan got a new top. He wanted to place it where it would be safe. He asked his dad to put it up high. Where can his dad put the top?

1. Write where Ryan's dad can put the top.

____

Draw a place Ryan's dad can put the top.

Comprehension: Yo-Yos

Directions: Read about yo-yos. Then, follow the instructions.

Yo-yo is a funny word. It means "come-come." Why? Move the yo-yo away from you on its string. It will come back!

1. Circle the main idea:

   You can move a yo-yo on a string.

   Yo-yo means "come-come" because it always comes back.

2. (Circle the correct answer.)
   A yo-yo moves:

3. Color the yo-yo.

Sequencing: Yo-Yo Trick

Directions: Read about the yo-yo trick.

Wind up the yo-yo string. Hold the yo-yo in your hand. Now, hold your palm up. Throw the yo-yo downward on the string. Hold your palm down. Now, swing the yo-yo forward. Make it "walk." This yo-yo trick is called "walk the dog."

Directions: Number the directions in order.

__________ Swing the yo-yo forward and make it "walk."

__________ Hold your palm up and drop the yo-yo.

__________ Turn your palm down as the yo-yo reaches the ground.

Comprehension: Sean's Basketball Game

Directions: Read about Sean's basketball game. Then, answer the questions.

Sean really likes to play basketball. One sunny day, he decided to ask his friends to play basketball at the park, but there were six people—Sean, Aki, Lance, Kate, Zac, and Oralia. A basketball team only allows five to play at a time. So, Sean decided to be the coach. Sean and his friends had fun.

1. How many kids wanted to play basketball? ____________

2. Write their names in ABC order:

   ____________ ____________ ____________

   ____________ ____________ ____________

3. How many players can play on a basketball team at a time? ____________

4. Where did they play basketball? ____________

5. Who decided to be the coach? ____________

Same/Different: Venn Diagram

A **Venn diagram** is a diagram that shows how two things are the same and different.

Directions: Choose two outdoor sports. Then, follow the instructions to complete the Venn diagram.

1. Write the first sport name under the first circle. Write some words that describe the sport. Write them in the first circle.

2. Write the second sport name under the second circle. Write some words that describe the sport. Write them in the circle.

3. Where the two circles overlap, write some words that describe both sports.

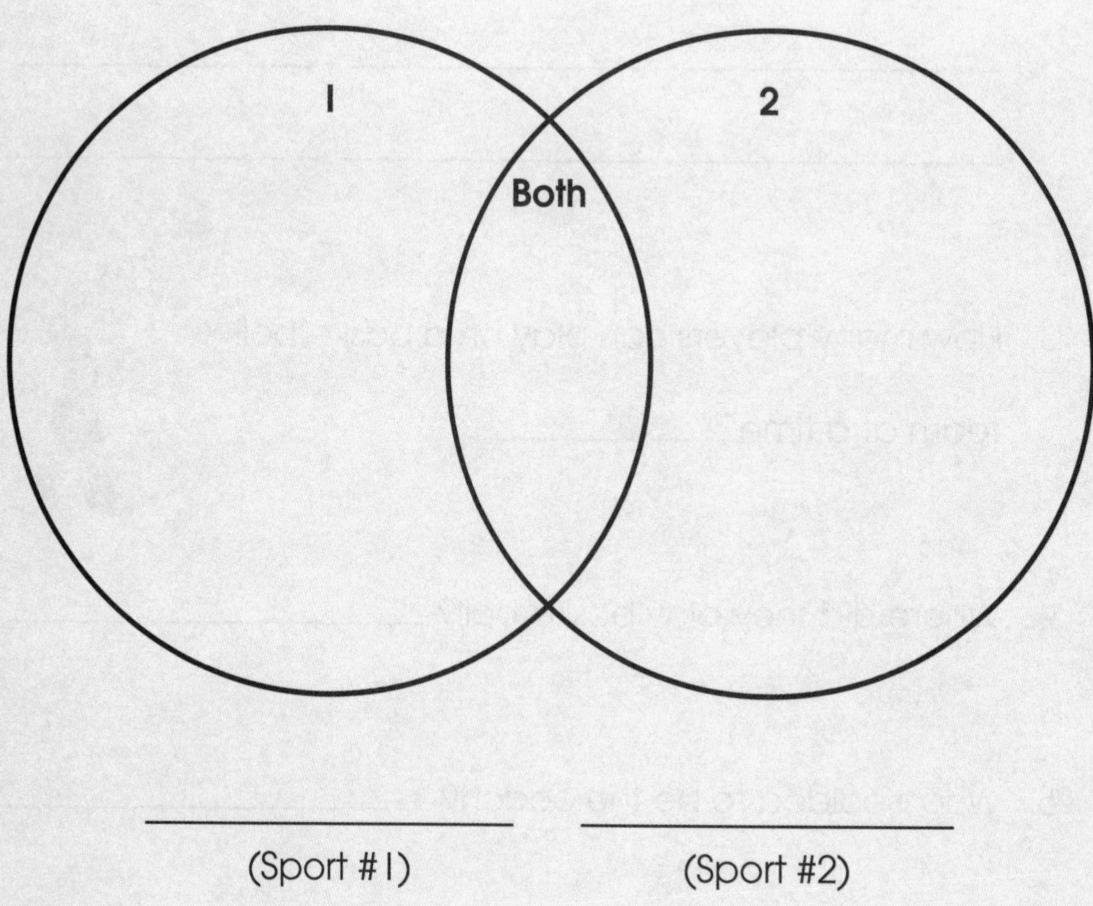

________________ (Sport #1)

________________ (Sport #2)

Comprehension: Carla and Tony Jump Rope

Directions: Read about jumping rope. Then, follow the instructions.

Carla and Tony like to jump rope. Carla likes to jump rope alone. Tony likes to have two people turn the rope for him. Carla and Tony can jump slowly. They can also jump fast.

1. Name another way to jump rope.

   a. Have two people turn the rope.

   b. ______________________________

   ____

2. Name two speeds for jumping rope.

   1) ______________________________

   2) ______________________________

3. Do you like to jump rope? ______________________________

   ____

Same/Different: Ann and Lee Have Fun

Directions: Read about Ann and Lee. Then, write how they are the same and different in the Venn diagram.

Ann and Lee like to play ball. They like to jump rope. Lee likes to play a card game called "Old Maid." Ann likes to play a card game called "Go Fish." What do you do to have fun?

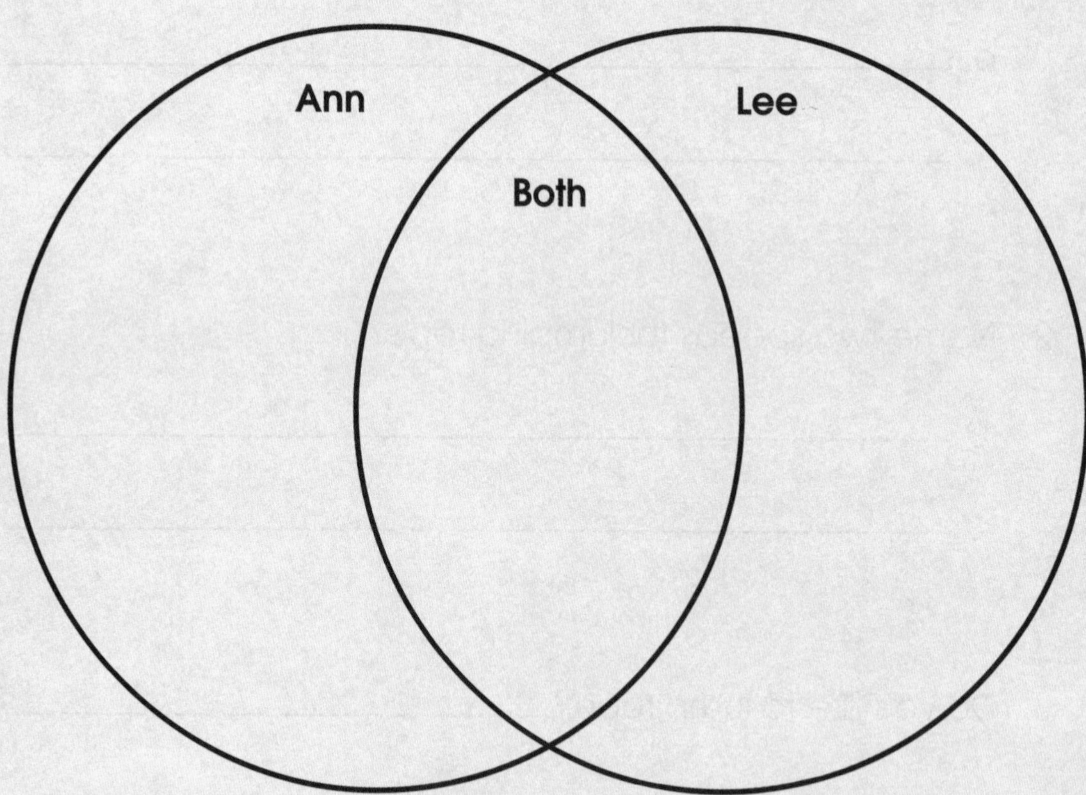

Predicting: A Rainy Game

Predicting is telling what is likely to happen based on the facts.

Directions: Read the story. Then, check each sentence below that tells how the story could end.

One cloudy day, Juan and his baseball team, the Bears, played the Crocodiles. It was the last half of the fifth inning, and it started to rain. The coaches and umpires had to decide what to do.

__________ They kept playing until nine innings were finished.

__________ Each player grabbed an umbrella and returned to the field to finish the game.

__________ They canceled the game and played it another day.

__________ They acted like crocodiles and slid around the wet bases.

__________ The coaches played the game while the players sat in the dugout.

Fiction/Nonfiction: Heavy Hitters

Fiction is a make-believe story. **Nonfiction** is a true story.

Directions: Read the stories about two famous baseball players. Then, write **fiction** or **nonfiction** in the baseball bats.

In 1998, Mark McGwire played for the St. Louis Cardinals. He liked to hit home runs. On September 27, 1998, he hit home run number 70, to set a new record for the most home runs hit in one season. The old record was set in 1961 by Roger Maris, who later played for the St. Louis Cardinals (1967 to 1968), when he hit 61 home runs.

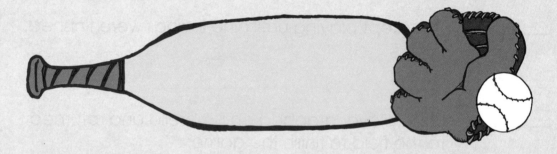

The Mighty Casey played baseball for the Mudville Nine and was the greatest of all baseball players. He could hit the cover off the ball with the power of a hurricane. But, when the Mudville Nine was behind 4 to 2 in the championship game, Mighty Casey struck out with the bases loaded. There was no joy in Mudville that day, because the Mudville Nine had lost the game.

Predicting: Oops!

Directions: Look at the pictures on the left. On the right, draw and write what you predict will happen next.

Fact and Opinion: Games!

A **fact** is something that can be proven. An **opinion** is a feeling or belief about something and cannot be proven.

Directions: Read these sentences about different games. Then, write **F** next to each fact and **O** next to each opinion.

_______ 1. Tennis is cool!

_______ 2. There are red and black markers in a Checkers game.

_______ 3. In football, a touchdown is worth six points.

_______ 4. Being a goalie in soccer is easy.

_______ 5. A yo-yo moves on a string.

_______ 6. June's sister looks like the queen on the card.

_______ 7. The six kids need three more players for a baseball team.

_______ 8. Table tennis is more fun than court tennis.

_______ 9. Play money is used in many board games.

Review

Directions: Read about ways to have fun. Then, follow the instructions.

There are many ways to have fun. You can bounce a ball. You can play with a yo-yo. You can jump rope. You can play a card game.

1. Circle the main idea:

   Jumping rope is fun.

   There are many ways to have fun.

2. Finish this list of ways to have fun.

   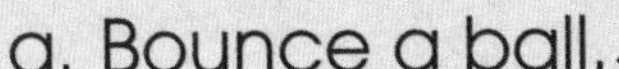

   a. Bounce a ball.

   b. ____________________

   c. ____________________

   d. ____________________

3. Circle the way these activities are the same:

   You use your hands to play them.

   Some are played inside.

4. Predict which activities kids will play when it is rainy and cold.

   ____

   ____

   ____

Recalling Details: Nikki's Pets

Directions: Read about Nikki's pets. Then, answer the questions.

Nikki has two cats, Tiger and Sniffer, and two dogs, Spot and Wiggles. Tiger is an orange striped cat who likes to sleep under a big tree and pretend she is a real tiger. Sniffer is a gray cat who likes to sniff the flowers in Nikki's garden. Spot is a Dalmatian with many black spots. Wiggles is a big furry brown dog who wiggles all over when he is happy.

1. Which dog is brown and furry? ________________

2. What color is Tiger? ________________

3. What kind of dog is Spot? ________________

4. Which cat likes to sniff flowers? ________________

5. Where does Tiger like to sleep? ________________

6. Who wiggles all over when he is happy? ________________

Predicting: KD Likes Milk

Directions: Read about KD the cat. Then, write what you think she will do.

KD likes milk. Perla, KD's owner, set out a pan of juice. Then, she set out a pan of milk.

1. What will KD do? ______________________________

____

____

2. Why? ______________________________

____

____

____

____

Comprehension: Playful Cats

Directions: Read about cats. Then, follow the instructions.

Cats make good pets. They like to play. They like to jump. They like to run. Do you?

1. (Circle the correct answer.) Cats make good

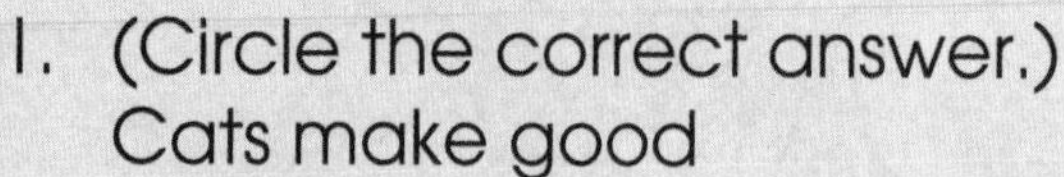

pets.

friends.

2. Write three things cats like to do.

1) ______________________________

2) ______________________________

3) ______________________________

3. Think of a good name for a cat. Write it on the cat's tag.

Predicting: What Will Bobby Do?

Directions: Read about Bobby the cat. Then, write what you think will happen.

One sunny spring day, Bobby was sleeping under her favorite tree. She was dreaming about her favorite food—tuna. Suddenly, she became hungry for a treat. Bobby woke up and listened when she heard someone call her name.

1. Why do you think Bobby was being called?

____

____

2. What do you think will happen next?

____

____

____

Sequencing/Predicting: A Game for Cats

Directions: Read about what cats like. Then, follow the instructions.

Cats like to play with paper bags. Pull a paper bag open. Take everything out. Now, lay it on its side.

1. Write 1, 2, and 3 to put the pictures in order.

2. In box 4, draw what you think the cat will do.

Same/Different: Marvin and Mugsy

Directions: Read about Marvin and Mugsy. Then, complete the Venn diagram, telling how they are the same and different.

Marcy has two dogs, Marvin and Mugsy. Marvin is a black-and-white spotted Dalmatian. Marvin likes to run after balls in the backyard. His favorite food is Canine Crunchy Crunch. Marcy likes to take Marvin for walks, because dogs need exercise. Marvin loves to sleep in his doghouse. Mugsy is a big furry brown dog, who wiggles when she is happy. Since she is big, she needs lots of exercise. So Marcy takes her for walks in the park. Her favorite food is Canine Crunchy Crunch. Mugsy likes to sleep on Marcy's bed.

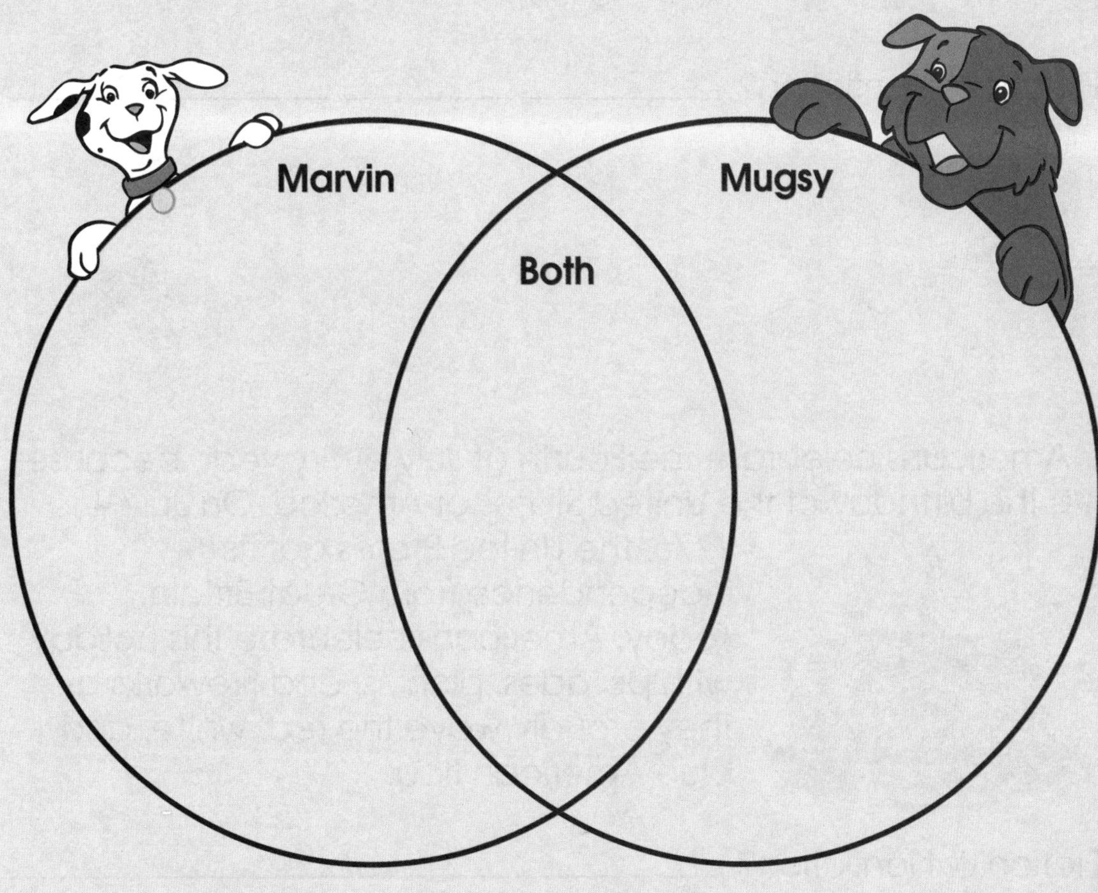

Fiction/Nonfiction: The Fourth of July

Directions: Read each story. Then, write whether it is fiction or nonfiction.

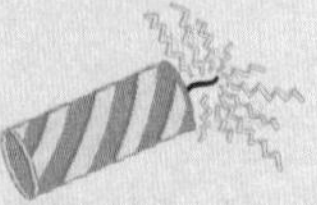

One sunny day in July, a dog named Stan ran away from home. He went up one street and down the other looking for fun, but all the yards were empty. Where was everybody?

Stan kept walking until he heard the sound of band music and happy people. Stan walked faster until he got to Central Street. There he saw men, women, children, and dogs getting ready to walk in a parade. It was the Fourth of July!

Fiction or Nonfiction? ______________________________

Americans celebrate the Fourth of July every year, because it is the birthday of the United States of America. On July 4,

1776, the United States got its independence from Great Britain. Today, Americans celebrate this holiday with parades, picnics, and fireworks as they proudly wave the red, white, and blue American flag.

Fiction or Nonfiction? ______________________________

Homophones: Doggy Birthday Cake

Homophones are words that sound alike but have different spellings and meanings.

Directions: Read the sentences. The bold words are homophones. Then, follow the directions for a doggy birthday cake.

1. The baker **read** a recipe to bake a doggy cake. Color the plate he put it on **red**.
2. Draw a **hole** in the middle of the doggy cake. Then, color the **whole** cake yellow.
3. Look **for** the top of the doggy cake. Draw **four** candles there.
4. In the hole, draw what you think the doggy would really like.

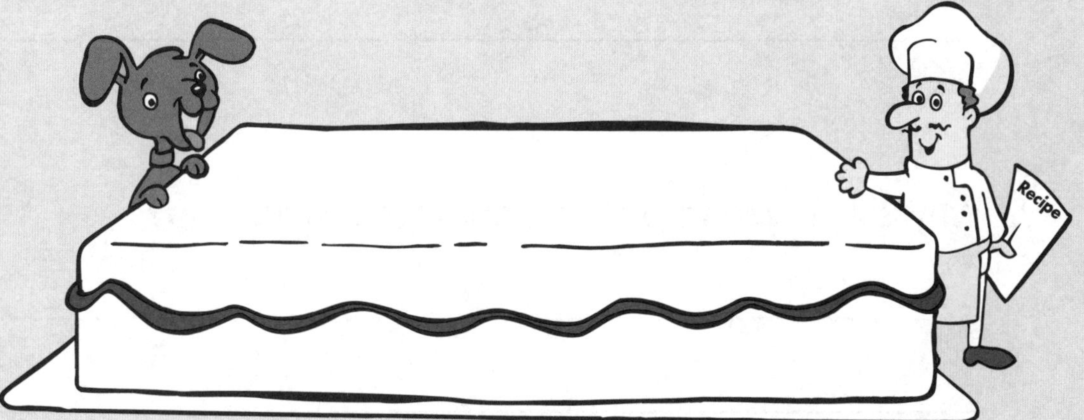

5. Write a sentence using the words **hole** and **whole**.

____

6. Write a sentence using the words **read** and **red**.

____

Comprehension: How to Stop a Dog Fight

Directions: Read about how to stop a dog fight. Then, answer the questions.

Sometimes dogs fight. They bark loudly. They may bite. Do not try to pull apart fighting dogs. Turn on a hose and spray them with water. This will stop the fight.

1. Name some things dogs may do if they are mad.

____

____

2. Why is it unwise to pull on dogs that are fighting?

____

____

3. Do you think dogs like to get wet?

____

____

Comprehension: Training a Dog

Directions: Read about how to train dogs. Then, answer the questions.

A dog has a ball in his mouth. You want the ball. What should you do? Do not pull on the ball. Hold out something else for the dog. The dog will drop the ball to take it!

1. Circle the main idea:

   Always get a ball away from a dog.

   Offer the dog something else to get him to drop the ball.

2. What should you not do if you want the dog's ball?

   ____

3. What could you hold out for the dog to take?

   ____

Comprehension: How to Meet a Dog

Directions: Read about how to meet a dog. Then, follow the instructions.

Do not try to pet a dog right away. First, let the dog sniff your hand. Do not move quickly. Do not talk loudly. Just let the dog sniff.

1. Predict what the dog will let you do if it likes you.

____

____

2. What should you let the dog do? ____________________

____

3. Name three things you should not do when you meet a dog.

1) ____

2) ____

3) ____

Comprehension: Dirty Dogs

Directions: Read about dogs. Then, answer the questions.

Like people, dogs get dirty. Some dogs get a bath once a month. Baby soap is a good soap for cleaning dogs. Fill a tub with warm water. Get someone to hold the dog still in the tub. Then, wash the dog fast.

1. How often do some dogs get a bath?

____

2. What is a good soap to use on dogs?

____

3. Do you think most dogs like to take baths?

____

Predicting: Dog-Gone!

Directions: Read the story. Then, follow the instructions.

Scotty and Simone were washing their dog, Willis. His fur was wet. Their hands were wet. Willis did not like to be wet. Scotty dropped the soap. Simone picked it up and let go of Willis. Uh-oh!

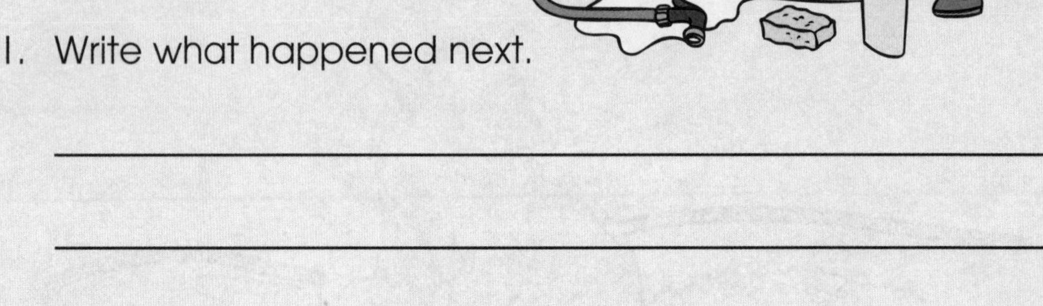

1. Write what happened next.

____

____

____

2. Draw what happened next.

Predicting: Dog Derby

Directions: Read the story. Then, answer the questions.

Marcy had a great idea for a game to play with her dogs, Marvin and Mugsy. The game was called "Dog Derby." Marcy would stand at one end of the driveway and hold on to the dogs by their collars. Her friend Mitch would stand at the other end of the driveway. When he said, "Go!" Marcy would let go of the dogs and they would race to Mitch. The first one there would get a dog biscuit. If there was a tie, both dogs would get a biscuit.

1. Who do you think will win the race?

   ____

   Why? ______________________________

   ____

2. What do you think will happen when they race again?

   ____

   ____

Recalling Details: Pet Pests

Directions: Read the story. Then, answer the questions.

Sometimes Marvin and Mugsy scratch and itch. Marcy knows that fleas or ticks are insect pests to her pets. Their bites are painful. Fleas suck the blood of animals. They don't have wings, but they can jump.Ticks are very flat, suck blood, and are related to spiders. They like to hide in dogs' ears. That is why Marcy checks Marvin and Mugsy every week for fleas and ticks.

1. What is a pest? ______________________________

____

2. List three facts about fleas.

   1) ______________________________________

   2) ______________________________________

   3) ______________________________________

3. List three facts about ticks.

   1) ______________________________________

   2) ______________________________________

   3) ______________________________________

Following Directions: Insect Art

Directions: Read about insects. Then, follow the instructions.

All insects have these body parts:

Head at the front

Thorax in the middle

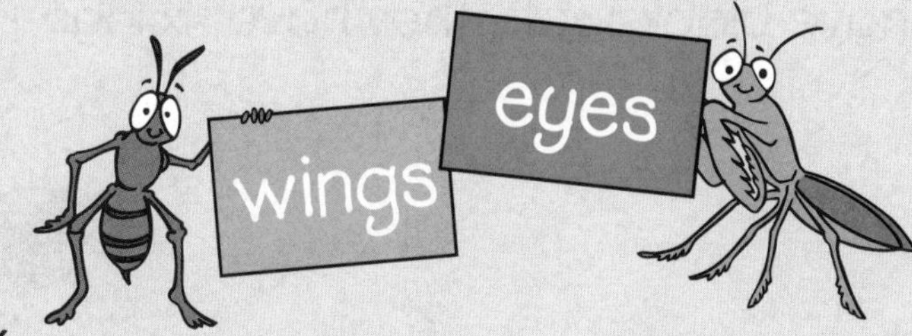

Abdomen at the back

Six **legs**—three on each side of the thorax

Two **eyes** on the head

Two **antennae** attached to the head

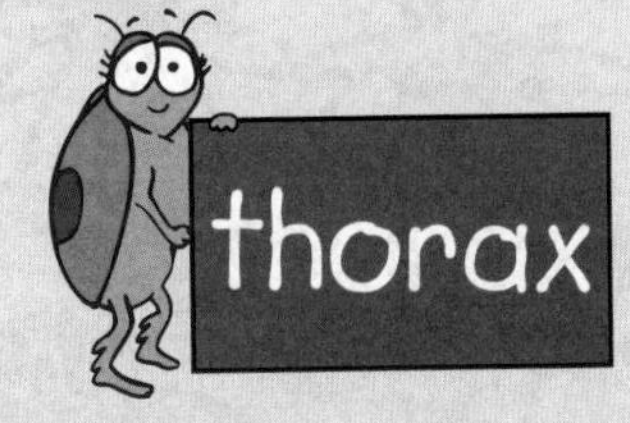

Some insects also have **wings**.

Draw your favorite insect. Include all the body parts listed above.

Comprehension: Ladybugs

Directions: Read about ladybugs. Then, answer the questions.

Have you ever seen a ladybug? Ladybugs are red. They have black spots. They have six legs. Ladybugs are pretty!

1. What color are ladybugs? ______________________

2. What color are their spots? ______________________

3. How many legs do ladybugs have? ______________________

Following Directions: How to Treat a Ladybug

Directions: Read about how to treat ladybugs. Then, follow the instructions.

Ladybugs are shy. If you see a ladybug, sit very still. Hold out your arm. Maybe the ladybug will fly to you. If it does, talk softly. Do not touch it. It will fly away when it is ready.

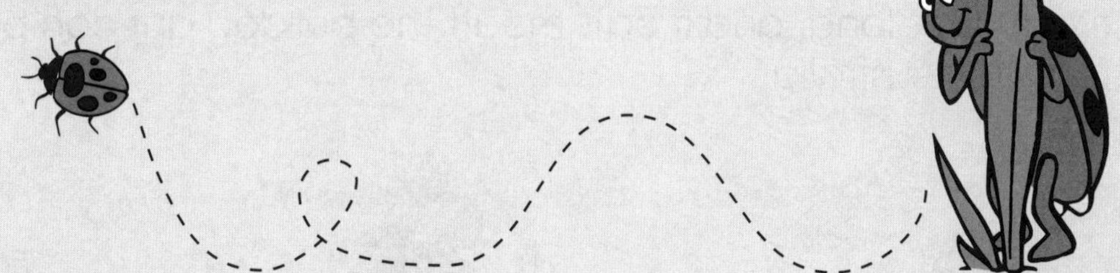

1. Complete the directions on how to treat a ladybug.

   a. Sit very still.

   b. ____________________

   c. Talk softly.

   d. ____________________

2. Ladybugs are **red**. They have **black** spots. Color the ladybug.

Comprehension: Amazing Ants

Directions: Read about ants. Then, answer the questions.

Ants are insects. Ants live in many parts of the world and make their homes in soil, sand, wood, and leaves. Most ants live for about six to 10 weeks. But the queen ant, who lays the eggs, can live for up to 15 years!

The largest ant is the bulldog ant. This ant can grow to be five inches long, and it eats meat! The bulldog ant can be found in Australia.

1. Where do ants make their homes? ______________________

____

2. How long can a queen ant live? ______________________

____

3. What is the largest ant? ______________________

4. What does it eat? ______________________

Comprehension: Ant Farms

Directions: Read about ant farms. Then, answer the questions.

Ant farms are sold at toy stores and pet stores. Ant farms come in a flat frame. The frame has glass on each side. Inside the glass is sand. The ants live in the sand.

1. Where are ant farms sold? ______________________________

2. The frame has ____________________________ on each side.

3. (Circle the correct answer.)
   The ants live in

   water.　　　　sand.

4. The ant farm frame is

   flat.　　　　round.

Making Inferences: Down on the Ant Farm

Directions: Read about ant farms. Then, answer the questions.

Ants are busy on the farm. They dig in the sand. They make roads in the sand. They look for food in the sand. When an ant dies, other ants bury it.

1. Where do you think ants are buried? ______________________

____

2. Is it fair to say ants are lazy? ______________________

3. Write a word that tells about ants. ______________________

Review

Directions: Read about goats. Then, answer the questions.

Goats make good pets. Like cows, goats give milk. Cows eat grass. Goats eat grass, too.

Here is how to make a goat your pet: Three days after it is born, take it from its mother. Then, feed it from a bottle. Hold it and pet it. The goat will think you are its mother.

1. What do both goats and cows eat? ____________________

2. Circle the main idea:

   Goats make good pets.

   Goats and cows eat grass.

3. Tell how to make a pet of your goat.

   a. Take it from its mother when it is three days old.

   b. ______________________________

   c. ______________________________

4. Why do you think the goat will think you are its mother?

   ____

Fact and Opinion: A Bounty of Birds

Directions: Read the story. Then, follow the instructions.

Tashi's family likes to go to the zoo. Her favorite animals are all the different kinds of birds. Tashi likes birds because they can fly, they have colorful feathers, and they make funny noises.

Write **F** next to each fact and **O** next to each opinion.

_______ 1. Birds have two feet.

_______ 2. All birds lay eggs.

_______ 3. Parrots are too noisy.

_______ 4. All birds have feathers and wings.

_______ 5. It would be great to be a bird and fly south for the winter.

_______ 6. Birds have hard beaks or bills instead of teeth.

_______ 7. Pigeons are fun to watch.

_______ 8. Some birds cannot fly.

_______ 9. A penguin is a bird.

Same/Different: Bluebirds and Parrots

Directions: Read about parrots and bluebirds. Then, complete the Venn diagram, telling how they are the same and different.

Bluebirds and parrots are both birds. Bluebirds and parrots can fly. They both have beaks. Parrots can live inside a cage. Bluebirds must live outdoors.

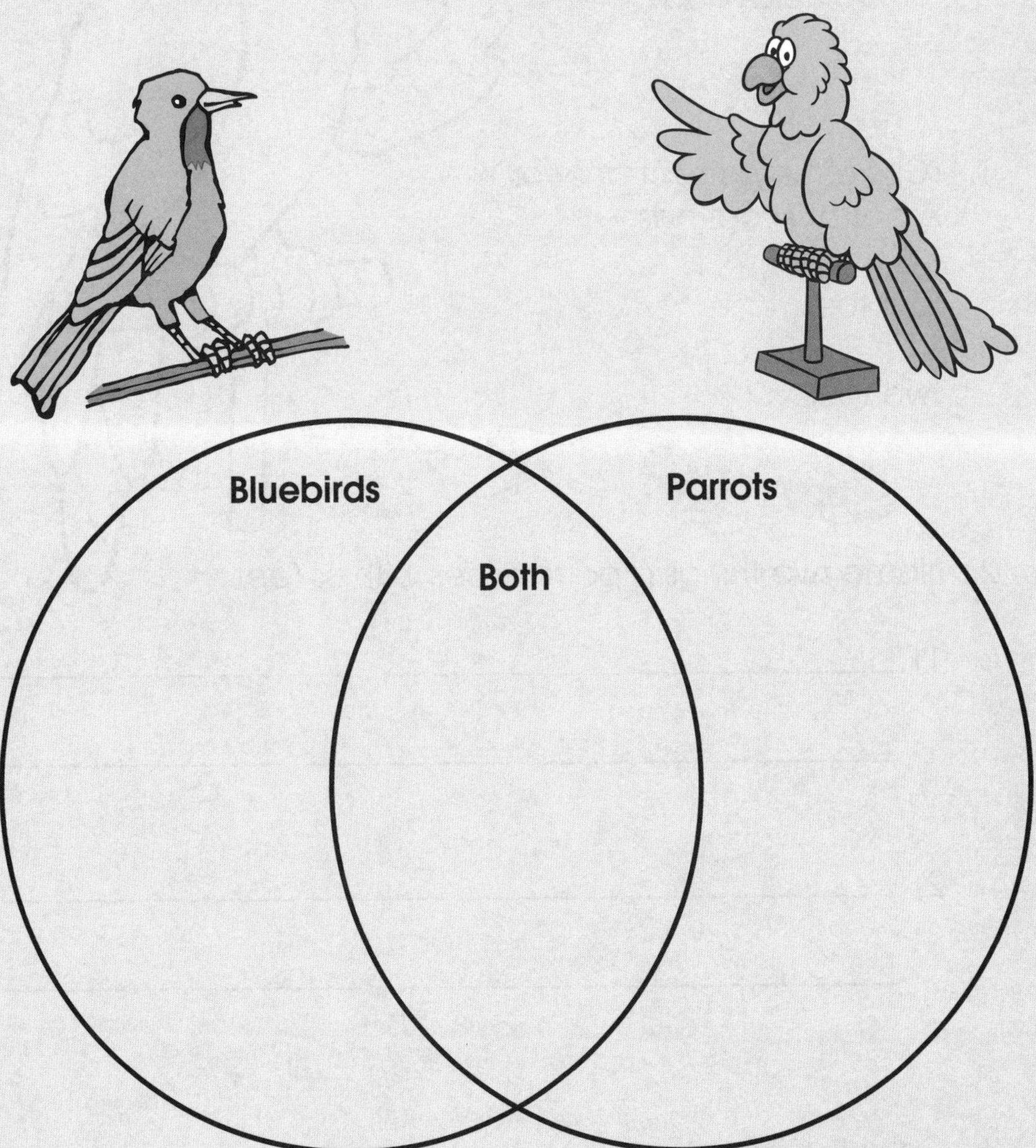

Comprehension: Pretty Parrots

Directions: Read about parrots. Then, follow the instructions.

Big parrots are pretty. Their feet have four toes each. Two toes are in front. Two toes are in back. Parrots use their feet to climb. They use them to hold food.

1. (Circle the correct answer.)
   A parrot's foot has

   four toes.

   two toes.

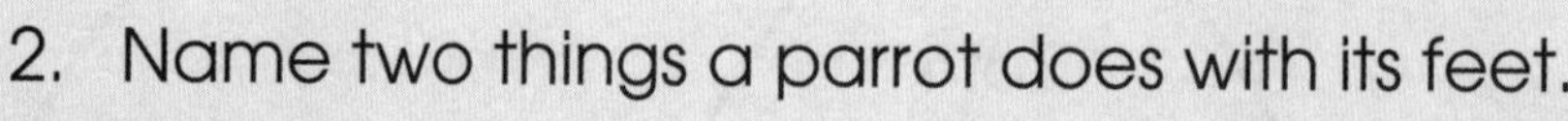

2. Name two things a parrot does with its feet.

   1) ______________________________

   ____

   2) ______________________________

   ____

3. Color the parrot.

Following Directions: Parrot Art

Directions: Draw the missing parts on each parrot.

1. Draw the parrot's eye.

2. Draw the parrot's tail.

3. Draw the parrot's beak.

4. Draw the parrot's wings.

Fact and Opinion: An Owl Story

Directions: Read the story. Then, follow the instructions.

My name is Owen Owl, and I am a bird. I go to Nocturnal School. Our teacher is Mr. Screech Owl. In his class, I learned that owls are birds, and can sleep all day and hunt at night. Some of us live in nests in trees. In North America, it is against the law to harm owls. I like being an owl!

Write **F** next to each fact and **O** next to each opinion.

_______ 1. No one can harm owls in North America.

_______ 2. It would be great if owls could talk.

_______ 3. Owls sleep all day.

_______ 4. Some owls sleep in nests.

_______ 5. Mr. Screech Owl is a good teacher.

_______ 6. Owls are birds.

_______ 7. Owen Owl would be a good friend.

_______ 8. Owls hunt at night.

_______ 9. Nocturnal School is a good school for smart owls.

Classifying: Carlos and Joshua's Bird Book

Directions: Read the story. Then, follow the instructions.

Carlos and Joshua learned that some birds like living near land and others like living near the water. They decided to write a book about land birds and water birds, but they needed some help. They looked in the library to find out which birds live near water and which birds live near land.

Read the bird names in the box. Then, list each bird under **Land** or **Water** to tell where it lives.

blue jay	cardinal	duck	goose
hummingbird	parrot	pelican	puffin
roadrunner	swan	eagle	penguin

Land	Water
1. ____________	1. ____________
2. ____________	2. ____________
3. ____________	3. ____________
4. ____________	4. ____________
5. ____________	5. ____________
6. ____________	6. ____________

Inferences: Monty's Trip

Directions: Read Monty's answer. Then, circle the answer to each question. Color the pictures.

Monty says, "I want to learn more about big cats. Someday, I would like to be an animal trainer or a zoo director. Where can we learn about big cats?"

1. What cat does Monty want to learn about?

2. Where should he go?

Sequencing: A Visit to the Zoo

Directions: Read the story. Then, follow the instructions.

One Saturday morning in May, Gloria and Anna went to the zoo. First, they bought tickets to get into the zoo. Second, they visited the Gorilla Garden and had fun watching the gorillas stare at them. Then, they went to Tiger Town and watched the tigers as they slept in the sunshine. Fourth, they went to Hippo Haven and laughed at the hippos cooling off in their pool. Next, they visited Snake Station and learned about poisonous and nonpoisonous snakes. It was noon, and they were hungry, so they ate lunch at the Parrot Patio.

Write **first, second, third, fourth, fifth,** and **sixth** to put the events in order.

_______________ They went to Hippo Haven.

_______________ Gloria and Anna bought zoo tickets.

_______________ They watched the tigers sleep.

_______________ They ate lunch at Parrot Patio.

_______________ The gorillas stared at them.

_______________ They learned about poisonous and nonpoisonous snakes.

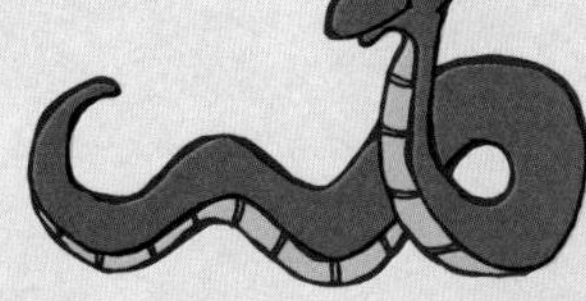

Recalling Details: Zoo Details

Directions: Reread "A Visit to the Zoo" on page 49. Then, follow the instructions.

1. Circle the main idea:

   Hippos are Anna and Gloria's favorite zoo animals.

   Tigers like to sleep in the sun.

   Anna and Gloria saw lots of animals at the zoo.

2. Write three details from the story about the hippos.

   1) ______________________________

   2) ______________________________

   3) ______________________________

Comprehension: Tigers

Directions: Read the story. Then, follow the instructions.

Tigers grow to be big! Some grow to be 10 feet long. Baby tigers are called cubs. They are small.

1. Circle the main idea:

   All tigers are big.

   Grown-up tigers are big. Baby tigers are small.

2. What is a baby tiger called? ______________________

3. Color the tigers.

Same/Different: Cats and Tigers

Directions: Read about cats and tigers. Then, complete the Venn diagram, telling how they are the same and different.

Tigers are a kind of cat. Pet cats and tigers both have fur. Pet cats are small and tame. Tigers are large and wild.

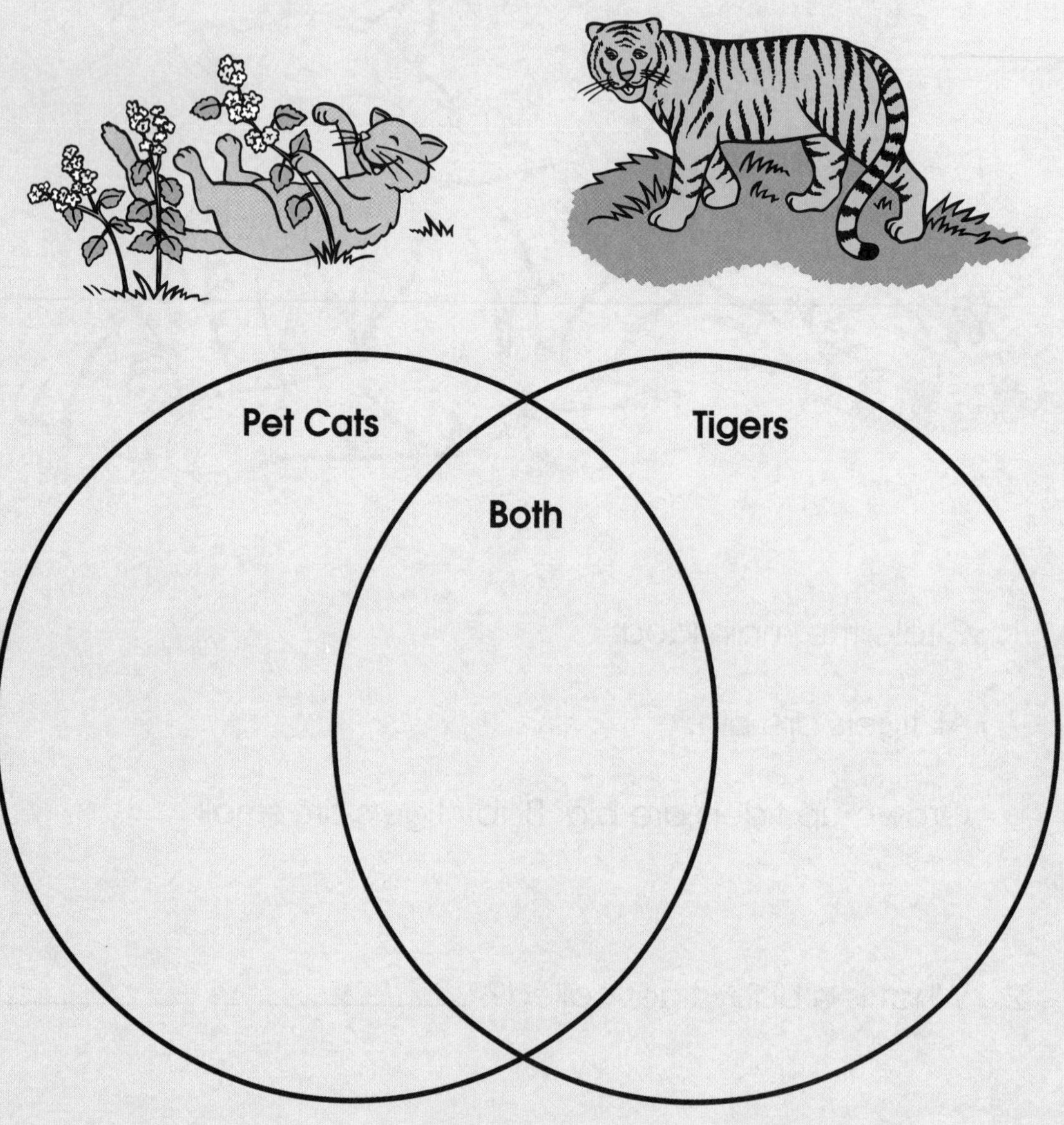

Comprehension: Snakes!

Directions: Read about snakes. Then, answer the questions.

There are many facts about snakes that might surprise someone. A snake's skin is dry. Most snakes are shy. They will hide from people. Snakes eat mice and rats. They do not chew them up. Snakes' jaws drop open to swallow their food whole.

1. How does a snake's skin feel? ______________________

2. Most snakes are ______________________.

3. What do snakes eat? 

   a. ______________________

   b. ______________________

Comprehension: More About Snakes!

Directions: Read more about snakes. Then, follow the instructions.

Unlike people, snakes have cold blood. They like to be warm. They hunt for food when it is warm. They lie in the sun. When it is cold, snakes curl up into a ball.

1. What do snakes do when it is warm?

   a. ______________________________

   b. ______________________________

2. Why do you think snakes curl up when it is cold?

   ____

   ____

3. (Circle the correct answer.)
   People have

   cold blood. warm blood.

Writing: My Snake Story

Directions: Write a fictional (make-believe) story about a snake. Make sure to include details and a title.

title

Review

Directions: Read about birds. Then, follow the instructions.

Birds use many things to make their nests. They use twigs. They use moss. Birds even use hair and yarn. You can help birds make a nest. First, cut up some yarn. Ask a grown-up to trim your hair. Then, put the yarn and hair outdoors.

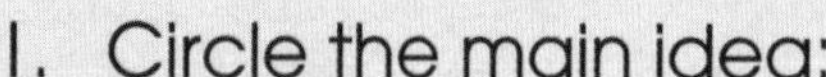

1. Circle the main idea:

   Cut your hair to help a bird.

   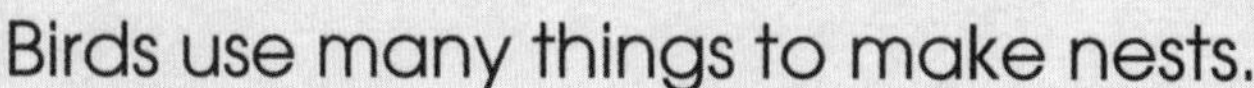

   Birds use many things to make nests.

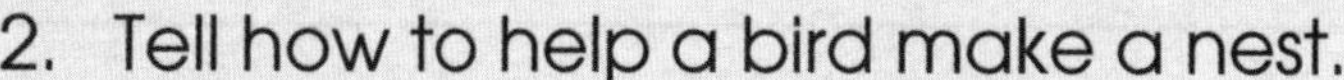

2. Tell how to help a bird make a nest.

   a. ______________________________

   b. ______________________________

   c. Put the yarn and hair outdoors.

3. Why do you think birds like yarn and hair?

   ____

4. Predict what birds will do with the yarn and hair.

   ____

Classifying: Animal Habitats

Directions: Read the story. Then, write each animal's name under **Water** or **Land** to tell where it lives.

Animals live in different habitats. A habitat is the place of an animal's natural home. Many animals live on land and others live in water. Most animals that live in water breathe with gills. Animals that live on land breathe with lungs.

fish	shrimp	giraffe	dog
cat	eel	whale	horse
bear	deer	shark	jellyfish

Water	**Land**
1. ______	1. ______
2. ______	2. ______
3. ______	3. ______
4. ______	4. ______
5. ______	5. ______
6. ______	6. ______

Comprehension: Sharks Are Fish, Too!

Directions: Read the story. Then, follow the instructions.

Angela learned a lot about sharks when her class visited the city aquarium. She learned that sharks are fish. Some sharks are as big as an elephant, and some can fit into a small paper bag. Sharks have no bones. They have hundreds of teeth, and when they lose them, they grow new ones. They eat animals of any kind. Whale sharks are the largest of all fish.

1. Circle the main idea:

   Angela learned a lot about sharks at the aquarium.

   Some sharks are as big as elephants.

2. When sharks lose teeth, they ______________________________

   ____.

3. ______________________________ are the largest of all fish.

4. (Circle the correct answer.)
   Sharks have bones.

   Yes   No

Comprehension: Fish

Directions: Read about fish. Then, follow the instructions.

Some fish live in warm water. Some live in cold water. Some fish live in lakes. Some fish live in oceans. There are 20,000 kinds of fish!

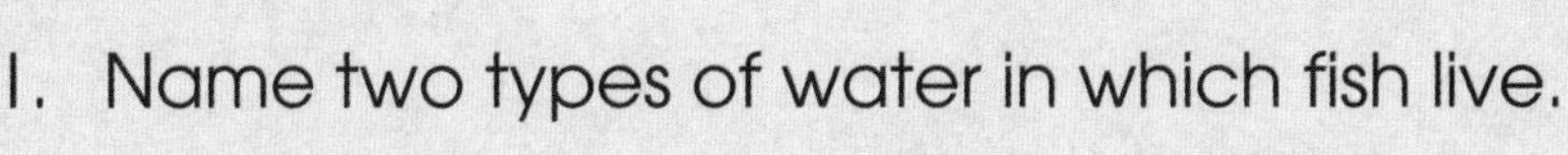

1. Name two types of water in which fish live.

   a. ______________________________

   b. ______________________________

2. Some fish live in lakes and some live in

   ______________________________ .

   Name another place fish live. ______________________________

3. There are ____________________ kinds of fish.

Comprehension: Fish Come in Many Colors

Directions: Read about the color of fish. Then, follow the instructions.

All fish live in water. Fish that live at the top are blue, green, or black. Fish that live down deep are silver or red. The colors make it hard to see the fish.

1. List the colors of fish at the top.

_______________ _______________ _______________

2. List the two colors of fish that live down deep.

_______________ _______________

3. Color the top fish and the bottom fish the correct colors.

Comprehension: Fish Can Protect Themselves

Directions: Read about two fish. Then, follow the instructions.

Most fish have ways to protect themselves from danger. Two of these fish are the trigger fish and the porcupine fish. The trigger fish lives on the ocean reef. When it sees danger, it swims into its private hole and puts its top fin up and squeezes itself in tight. Then, it cannot be taken from its hiding place. The porcupine fish also lives on the ocean reef. When danger comes, it puffs up like a balloon by swallowing air or water. When it puffs up, poisonous spikes stand out on its body. When danger is past, it deflates its body.

1. Circle the main idea:

   Trigger fish and porcupine fish can be dangerous.

   Some fish have ways to protect themselves from danger.

2. Trigger fish and porcupine fish live on the

   ____ .

3. The porcupine fish puffs up by swallowing

   ____________________ or ____________________ .

Predicting: Puff and Trigg

Directions: Read about Puff and Trigg. Then, write what happens next in the story.

It was a sunny, warm day in the Pacific Ocean. Puff, the happy porcupine fish, and Trigg, the jolly trigger fish, were having fun playing fish tag. They were good friends. Suddenly, they saw the shadow of a giant fish! It was coming right at them! They knew the giant fish might like eating smaller fish! What did they do?

What did Puff and Trigg do to get away from the giant fish?

____

____

____

____

____

____

____

Making Inferences: Just Ducky

Directions: Read about ducks. Then, answer the questions.

Ducks have wide feet. They use them to swim. Ducks move their feet under water.

1. Why do ducks move their feet under water?

____

2. A duck's feet look ______________________________________ .

3. Color the duck's feet orange.

Comprehension: Ducks in the Park

Directions: Read about ducks in the park. Then, follow the instructions.

Have you ever been to a park? Did you see baby ducks? Baby ducks can swim and walk. They can find their own food.

1. Circle the main idea:

   You can go to a park.

   Baby ducks can do many things.

2. List what baby ducks can do.

   a. ____________________

   b. ____________________

   c. ____________________

3. What would you name a baby duck?

   ____

Same/Different: Dina and Dina

Directions: Read the story. Then, complete the Venn diagram, telling how Dina, the duck, is the same or different than Dina, the girl.

One day in the library, Dina found a story about a duck named Dina!

My name is Dina. I am a duck, and I like to swim. When I am not swimming, I walk on land or fly. I have two feet and two eyes. My feathers keep me warm. Ducks can be different colors. I am gray, brown, and black. I really like being a duck. It is fun.

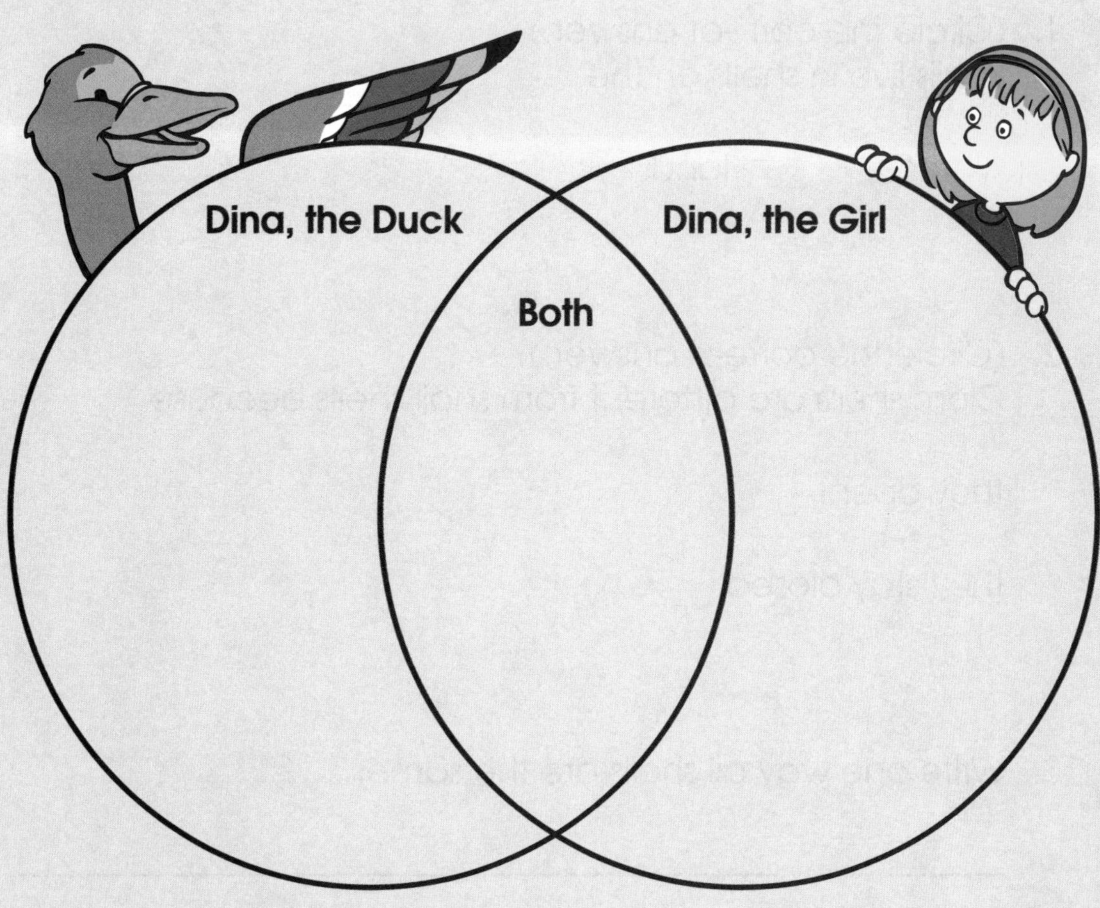

Same/Different: Shell Homes

Directions: Read about shells. Then, answer the questions.

Shells are the homes of some animals. Snails live in shells on the land. Clams live in shells in the water. Clam shells open. Snail shells stay closed. Both shells keep the animals safe.

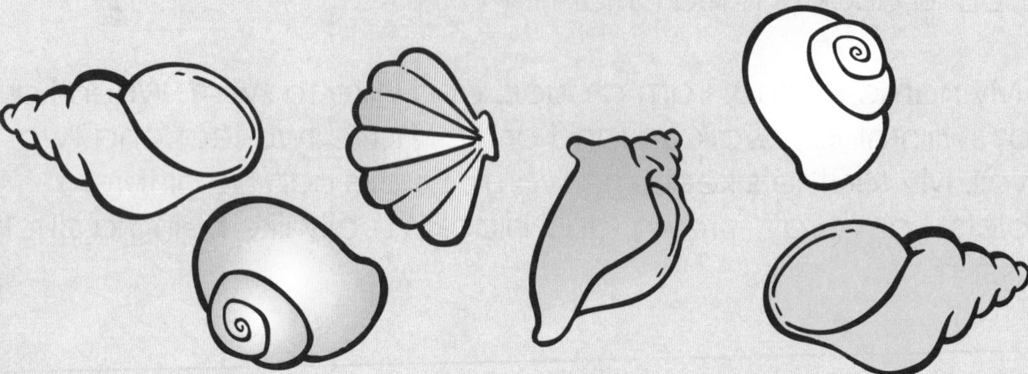

1. (Circle the correct answer.)
   Snails live in shells on the

   water. land.

2. (Circle the correct answer.)
   Clam shells are different from snail shells because

   they open.

   they stay closed.

3. Write one way all shells are the same.

   ____

   ____

Comprehension: Sea Horses Look Strange!

Directions: Read about sea horses. Then, answer the questions.

Sea horses are fish, not horses. A sea horse's head looks like a horse's head. It has a tail like a monkey's tail. A sea horse looks very strange!

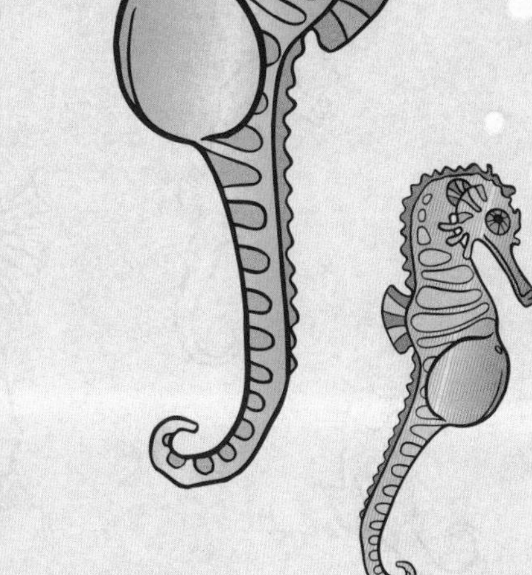

1. (Circle the correct answer.) A sea horse is a kind of

   horse.

   monkey.

   fish.

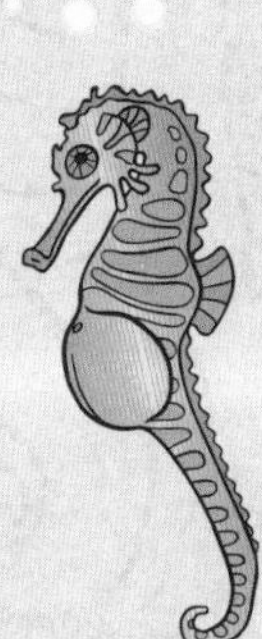

2. What does a sea horse's head look like?

   ____

   ____

3. What makes a sea horse look strange?

   a. ______________________________

   b. ______________________________

Making Inferences: More About Sea Horses

Directions: Read more about sea horses. Then, answer the questions.

A father sea horse helps the mother. He has a small sack, or pouch, on the front of his body. The mother sea horse lays the eggs. She does not keep them. She gives the eggs to the father.

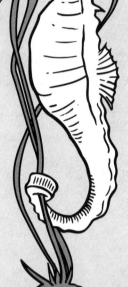

1. What does the mother sea horse do with her eggs?

____

2. Where does the father sea horse put the eggs?

____

3. Sea horses can change color. Color the sea horses.

Comprehension: Singing Whales

Directions: Read about singing whales. Then, follow the instructions.

Some whales can sing! We cannot understand the words. But we can hear the tune of the humpback whale. Each season, humpback whales sing a different song.

1. Circle the main idea:

   All whales can sing.

   Some whales can sing.

2. Name the kind of whale that sings.

   ____

3. How many different songs does the humpback whale sing each year?

   1 2 3 4

Same/Different: Sleeping Whales

Directions: Read more about whales. Then, complete the Venn diagram, telling how whales and people are the same and different.

Whales do not sleep like we do. They take many short naps. Like us, whales breathe air. Whales live in very cold water, but they have fat that keeps them warm.

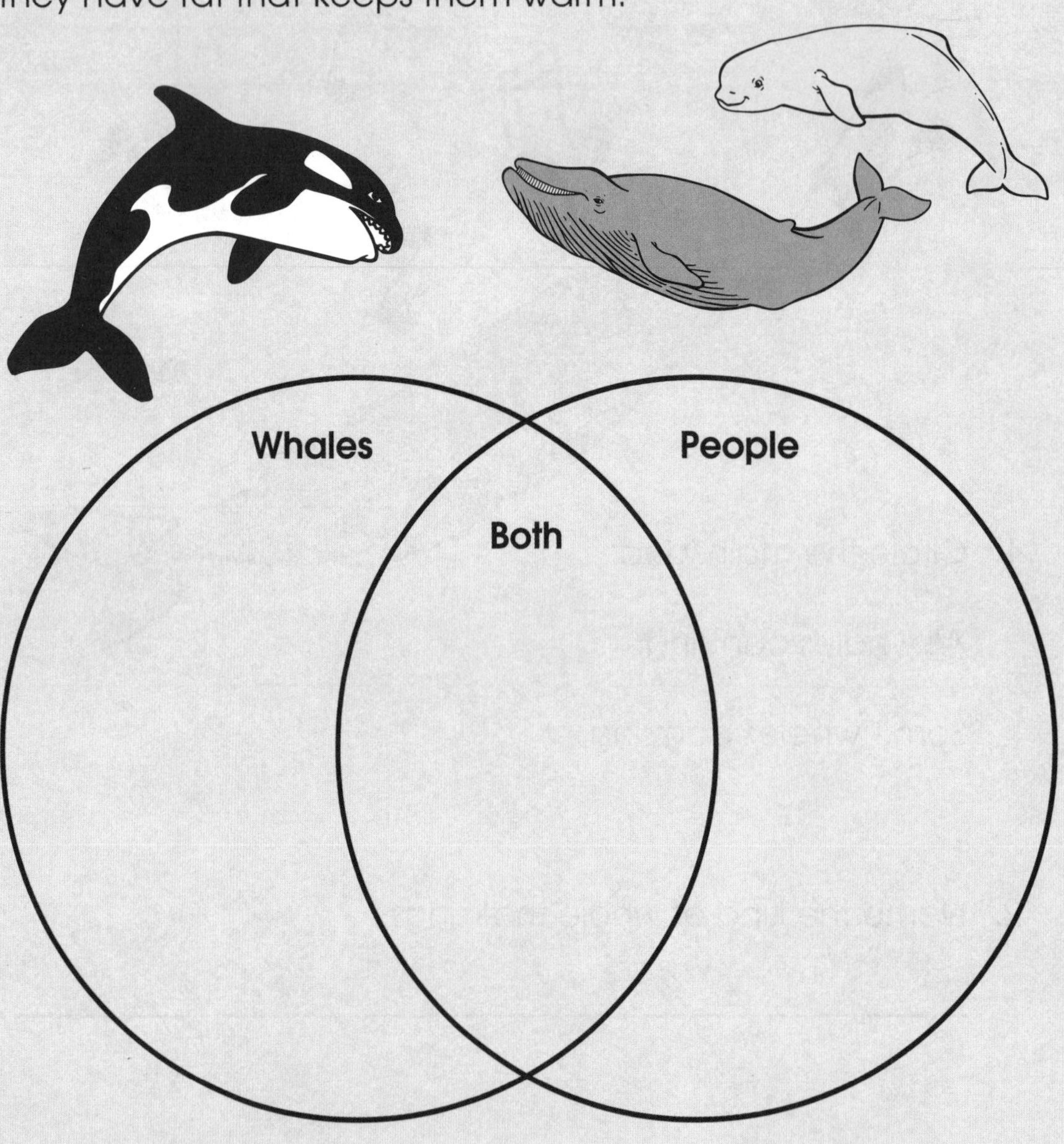

Fact and Opinion: Henrietta the Humpback

Directions: Read the story. Then, follow the instructions.

My name is Henrietta, and I am a humpback whale. I live in cold seas in the summer and warm seas in the winter. My long flippers are used to move forward and backward. I like to eat fish. Sometimes, I show off by leaping out of the water. Would you like to be a humpback whale?

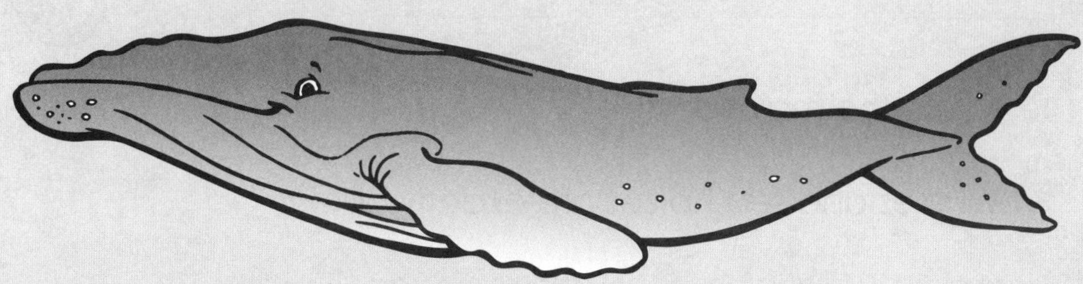

Write **F** next to each fact and **O** next to each opinion.

_______ 1. Being a humpback whale is fun.

_______ 2. Humpback whales live in cold seas during the summer.

_______ 3. Whales are fun to watch.

_______ 4. Humpback whales use their flippers to move forward and backward.

_______ 5. Henrietta is a great name for a whale.

_______ 6. Leaping out of water would be hard.

_______ 7. Humpback whales like to eat fish.

Review

Directions: Read about whales and sea horses. Then, follow the instructions.

Whales and sea horses both live in the ocean. Sea horses grow to be about six inches long. Whales can grow to be 100 feet long. Sea horses swim with their heads up and tails down. Whales swim on their bellies.

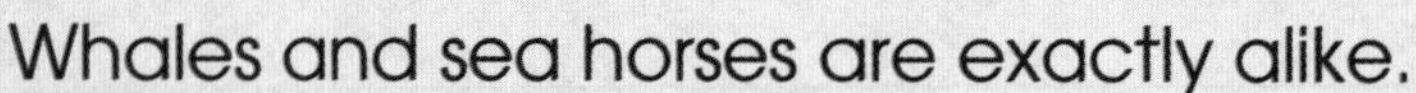

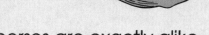

1. Circle the main idea:

   Whales and sea horses are exactly alike.

   Whales and sea horses are very different.

2. Write one way whales and sea horses are the same.

   ____

3. On another sheet of paper, complete a Venn diagram telling how whales and sea horses are the same and different.

4. (Circle the correct answer.)
   Predict whether whales would be afraid of sea horses.

   Yes   No

Comprehension: Do You Like Jokes?

Directions: Read about jokes. Then, answer the questions.

Most kids like **jokes**. Some jokes are long. Some jokes are short. Good jokes are funny. Do you know a funny joke?

1. Circle the main idea:

   There are many kinds of jokes.

   Some jokes are short.

2. Write a definition for **joke**.

   ____

   ____

   ____

   ____

Making Inferences: Jake's Jokes and Riddles

Directions: Read the story. Then, tell the jokes using the picture words.

Jake likes to tell funny jokes and riddles. A joke is something that is said, done, or written to make someone laugh. A riddle is a question that has a tricky answer. Jake writes riddles and jokes using pictures in place of words or letters.

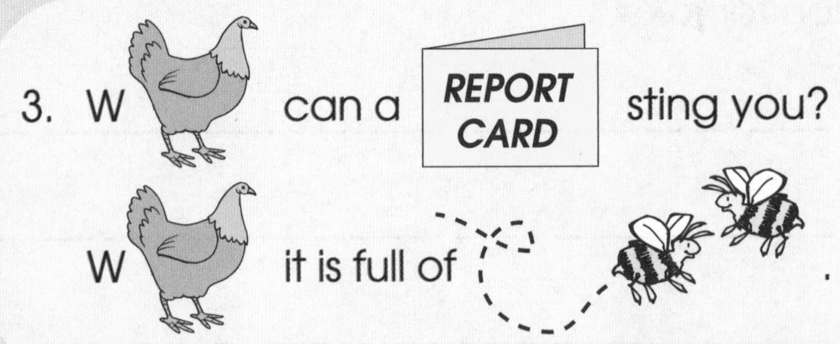

3. W can a
REPORT
CARD
sting you?
W it is full of .

Comprehension: Letter Jokes

Directions: Draw the answers to the jokes. Then, write a joke you know.

Here are some jokes about letters.

What letter is part of the face? **I** (eye).

What letter can buzz? **B** (bee).

1. Draw the answer to the letter **I** joke.

2. Draw the answer to the letter **B** joke.

3. Write a joke you know.

Making Inferences: Color and Number Jokes

Directions: Read about jokes. Then, answer the questions.

Here are more jokes! Do you know what color is loud? Do you know what number is not hungry?

1. (Circle the correct answer.)
   The color that is loud is:

   Purple Yellow

2. The number that is not hungry is:

   Eight Two

3. Here is one more joke:
   What color do you say when you are done with a book?

   "I have ______________________________ it all."

Fiction: Hercules

The setting is where a story takes place. The characters are the people in a story or play.

Directions: Read about Hercules. Then, answer the questions.

Hercules was born in the warm Atlantic Ocean. He was a very small and weak baby. He wanted to be the strongest hurricane in the world. But he had one problem. He couldn't blow 75-mile-per-hour winds. Hercules blew and blew in the ocean, until one day, his sister, Hola, told him it would be more fun to be a breeze than a hurricane. Hercules agreed. It was a breeze to be a breeze!

1. What is the setting of the story? ____________________

2. Who are the characters? ____________________

3. What is the problem? ____________________

4. How does Hercules solve his problem? ____________________

Nonfiction: Tornado Tips

Directions: Read about tornadoes. Then, follow the instructions.

A tornado begins over land with strong winds and thunderstorms. The spinning air becomes a funnel. It can cause damage. If you are inside, go to the lowest floor of the building. A basement is a safe place. A bathroom or closet in the middle of a building can be a safe place, too. If you are outside, lie in a ditch. Remember, tornadoes are dangerous.

Write five facts about tornadoes.

1. ____

2. ____

3. ____

4. ____

5. ____

Comprehension: A Winter Story

Directions: Read about winter. Then, follow the instructions.

It is cold in winter. Snow falls. Water freezes. Most kids like to play outdoors. Some kids make a snowman. Some kids skate. What do you do in winter?

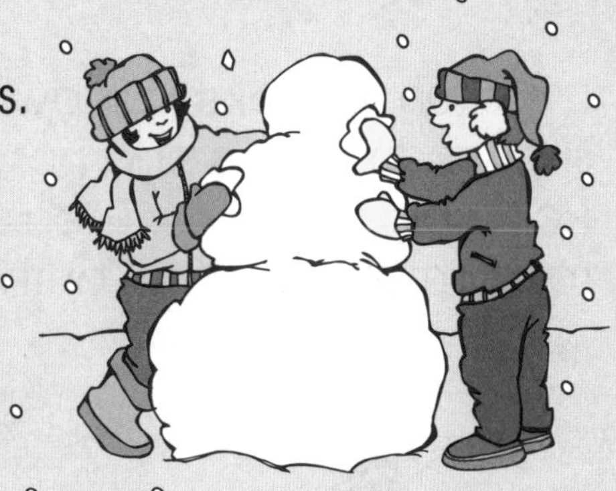

1. Circle the main idea:

   Snow falls in winter.

   In winter, there are many things to do outside.

2. Write two things about winter weather.

   1) ______________________________

   2) ______________________________

3. Write what you like to do in winter.

____

____

____

____

____

Sequencing: Making a Snowman

Directions: Read about how to make a snowman. Then, follow the instructions.

It is fun to make a snowman. First, find things for the snowman's eyes and nose. Dress warmly. Then, go outdoors. Roll a big snowball. Then, roll another to put on top of it. Now, roll a small snowball for the head. Put on the snowman's face.

1. Number the pictures in order.

2. Write two things to do before going outdoors.

    1) ______________________________

    2) ______________________________

Classifying: A Rainy Day

Directions: Read the story. Then, circle the objects Jonathan needs to stay dry.

It is raining. Jonathan wants to play outdoors. What should he wear to stay dry? What should he carry to stay dry?

Sequencing: Why Does it Rain?

Directions: Read about rain. Then, follow the instructions.

Clouds are made up of little drops of ice and water. They push and bang into each other. Then, they join together to make bigger drops and begin to fall. More raindrops cling to them. They become heavy and fall quickly to the ground.

Write **first**, **second**, **third**, **fourth**, and **fifth** to put the events in order.

________________ More raindrops cling to them.

________________ Clouds are made up of little drops of ice and water.

________________ They join together and make bigger drops that begin to fall.

________________ The drops of ice and water bang into each other.

________________ The drops become heavy and fall quickly to the ground.

Comprehension: Playing Store

Directions: Read about playing store. Then, answer the questions.

Tyson and his friends like to play store. They use boxes and cans. They line them up. Then, they put them in bags.

1. Circle the main idea:

   Tyson and his friends use boxes, cans, and bags to play store.

   You need bags to play store.

2. (Circle the correct answer.)
   Who likes to play store?

   all kids some kids

3. Do you like to play store? ______________________________

Sequencing: Packing Bags

Directions: Read about packing bags. Then, number the objects in the order they should be packed.

Cans are heavy. Put them in first. Then, put in boxes. Now, put in the apple. Put the bread in last.

Sequencing: Baking a Cake

Directions: Read about baking a cake. Then, write the missing steps.

Dylan, Dana, and Dad are baking a cake. Dad turns on the oven. Dana opens the cake mix. Dylan adds the eggs. Dad pours in the water. Dana stirs the batter. Dylan pours the batter into a cake pan. Dad puts it in the oven.

1. Turn on the oven.

2. ______________________________

3. Add the eggs.

4. ______________________________

5. Stir the batter.

6. ______________________________

7. ______________________________

Making Deductions: A Menu

Directions: Look at the clues below. Fill in the menu.

Sunday ____________

Monday ____________

Tuesday ____________

Wednesday ____________

Thursday ____________

Friday ____________

Saturday ____________

1. Mom fixed stew on Monday.
2. Dad fixed chef salad the day before that.
3. Lila made a potpie three days after Mom fixed stew.
4. Ross fixed corn-on-the-cob the day before Lila made potpie.
5. Mom fixed pizza the day after Lila made the potpie.
6. Lila cooked fish the day before Dad fixed chef salad.
7. Dad is making chicken today. What day is it?

____

Prefixes: The Three R's

Prefixes are syllables added to the beginning of words that change their meaning. The prefix **re** means "again."

Directions: Read the story. Then, follow the instructions.

Kim wants to find ways she can save Earth. She studies the "three R's" —reduce, reuse, and recycle. Reduce means to make less. Both reuse and recycle mean to use again.

Add **re** to the beginning of each word below. Use the new words to complete the sentences.

________ build	________ fill	________ write
________ read	________ tell	________ run

1. The race was a tie, so Dawn and Kathy had to ________________ it.
2. The block wall fell down, so Simon had to ________________ it.
3. The water bottle was empty, so Luna had to ________________ it.
4. Javier wrote a good story, but he wanted to ________________ it to make it better.
5. The teacher told a story, and students had to ________________ it.
6. Toni didn't understand the directions, so she had to ________________ them.

Review

Directions: Read the story. Then, follow the instructions.

The cake is done. Dad takes it from the oven. Dylan and Dana want to frost the cake. "I want to use white frosting," says Dylan. "I want to use red frosting," says Dana. "We will use both your ideas," says Dad. "We will have pink frosting!"

1. Circle the main idea:

   The cake will have red frosting.

   Pink frosting is made of red and white frosting.

2. (Circle the correct answer.)
   The cake is frosted

   after it is taken from the oven.

   before it is taken from the oven.

3. Write directions for making pink frosting.

   ____

   ____

   ____

Classifying: Art Tools

Directions: Read about art tools. Then, color only the art tools.

Andrea uses different art tools to help her design her masterpieces. To cut, she needs scissors. To draw, she needs a pencil. To color, she needs crayons. To paint, she needs a brush.

Write which tools are needed to:

draw	color	cut
______________	______________	______________

Classifying: Find the Puppets

Directions: Read about puppets. Then, follow the instructions.

There are many kinds of puppets. Puppets can be made from paper bags, socks, mittens, cardboard tubes, and plastic cups. Some puppets fit on your hand. Some puppets fit on your fingers. Some puppets are moved by string.

1. Find and circle the three puppets below.

2. What kinds of puppets did you find?

____

____

____

Predicting: A Pair of Puppets

Directions: Read the story. Then, answer the questions.

Pablo and Paki are a pair of puppets who belong to Rosie. She uses them in her puppet plays at school. Her friends have fun playing with them, too. One day, Brandon, a new boy in the class, hid Pablo and Paki in his desk. No one could find them. Rosie and her friends were very sad.

1. What do you think Rosie will do? ______________________

____

2. What do you think Brandon will do? ____________________

____

3. What do you think Pablo and Paki will do? ______________

____

Comprehension: Paper-Bag Puppets

Directions: Read about paper-bag puppets. Then, follow the instructions.

It is easy to make a hand puppet. You need a small paper bag. You need colored paper. You need glue. You need scissors. Are you ready?

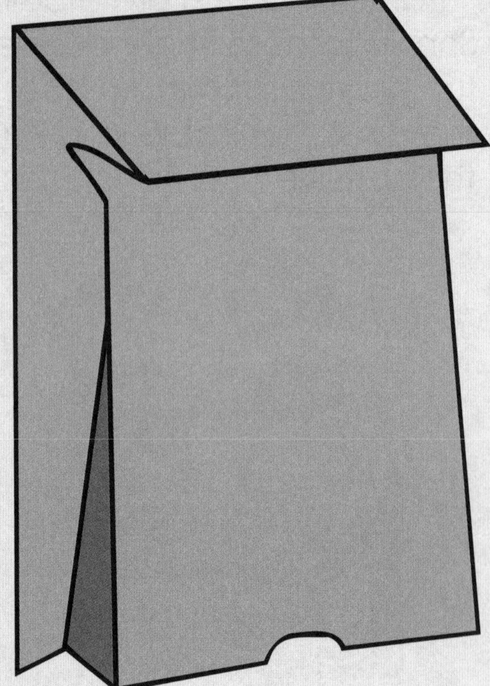

1. Circle the main idea:

   You need scissors.

   Making a hand puppet is easy.

2. Write the four objects you need to make a paper-bag puppet.

   1) ______________________________

   2) ______________________________

   3) ______________________________

   4) ______________________________

3. Draw a face on the paper-bag puppet.

Sequencing: Make a Paper-Bag Puppet

Directions: Read about how to make a paper-bag puppet. Then, answer the questions.

Find a small paper bag that fits your hand. Make a face where the bag folds. Cut out teeth from colored paper. Glue them on the bag. Make ears. Make a nose. Make a mouth. Glue them on the bag.

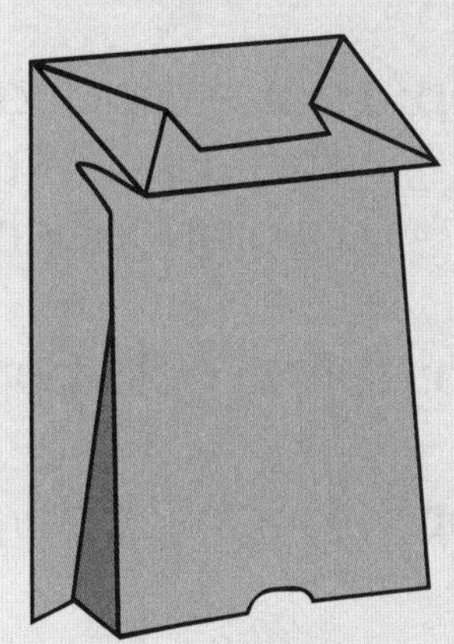

1. What will you cut out first? ______________________________

2. What will you cut out last? ______________________________

3. Number the steps in order.

Comprehension: The Puppet Play

Directions: Read the play out loud with a friend. Then, answer the questions.

Pip: Hey, Pep. What kind of turkey eats very fast?

Pep: Uh, I don't know.

Pip: A gobbler!

Pep: I have a good joke for you, Pip. What kind of burger does a polar bear eat?

Pip: Uh, a cold burger?

Pep: No, an iceberg-er!

Pip: Hey, that was a great joke!

1. Who are the characters in the play? ____________________

____

2. Who are the jokes about? ____________________

____

3. What are the characters in the play doing? ____________________

____

Comprehension: Making New Cards From Old

Directions: Read about making cards. Then, answer the questions.

Did you ever get a card? Do you still have it? Sonia uses old cards to make new cards. Then, she can recycle the old card and give the new card to a special friend.

1. What can you use to make a new card? ______________

____

2. What can you do with the new card? ______________

____

3. Who can you give a card to? ______________

____

Sequencing: Making a Card

Directions: Read about how to make a card. Then, follow the instructions.

You will need scissors, glue, and colored paper. First, look at all your old cards. Then, cut out what you like. Now, fold the colored paper in half. Glue the cut-outs to the front of your card. Write your name inside.

1. Write the steps in order for making a card.

   1) Look at all your old cards.

   2) ________________________________

   3) ________________________________

   4) ________________________________

2. Write your name inside.

3. Draw a picture of a new card you could make.

Comprehension: Just Junk?

Directions: Read about saving things. Then, follow the instructions.

Do you save old crayons? Do you save old buttons or cards? Some people call these things junk. They throw them out. Leah saves these things. She likes to use them for art projects. She puts them in a box. What do you do?

1. Circle the main idea:

   Everyone has junk.

   People have different ideas about what junk is.

2. Name two kinds of junk.

   1) ______________________________

   2) ______________________________

3. What are two things you can do with old things?

   1) ______________________________

   2) ______________________________

Following Directions: Color the Junk

Directions: Color the buttons **red**. Color the jacks **silver**. Color the crayons **green**. Then, draw and color some of the things you save.

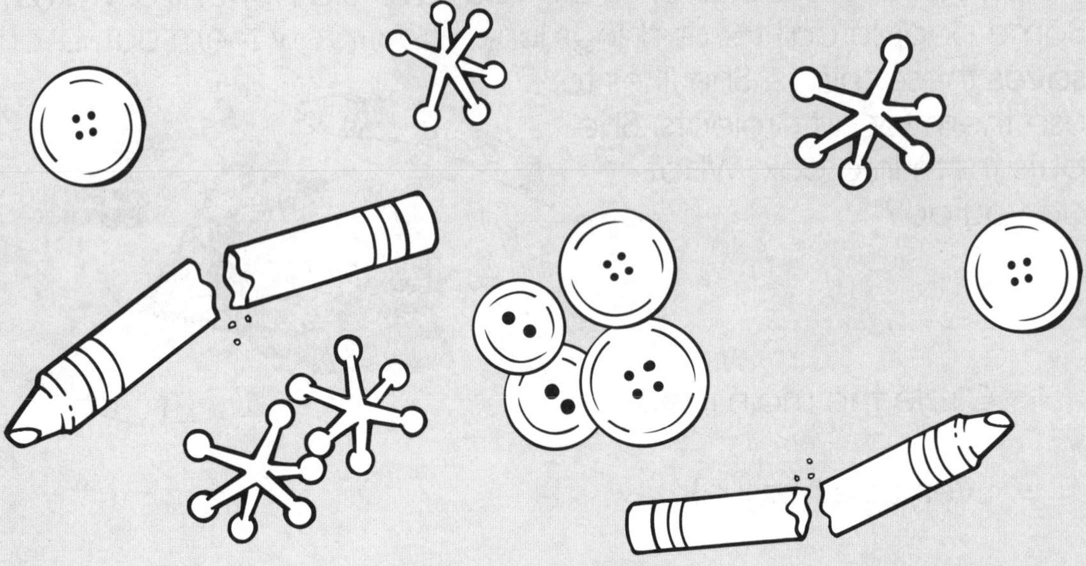

Sequencing: Make a Pencil Holder

Directions: Read how to make a pencil holder. Then, follow the instructions.

You can use "junk" to make a pencil holder! First, you need a clean can with one end removed. Make sure there are no sharp edges. Then, you need glue, scissors, and paper. Find colorful paper such as wrapping paper, wallpaper, or construction paper. Cut the paper to fit the can. Glue the paper around the can. Decorate your can with glitter, buttons, and stickers. Then, put your pencils inside!

Write **first, second, third, fourth, fifth, sixth,** and **seventh** to put the steps in order.

________________ Make sure there are no sharp edges.

________________ Get glue, scissors, and paper.

________________ Cut the paper to fit the can.

________________ Put your pencils in the can!

________________ Glue colorful paper to the can.

________________ Remove one end of a clean can.

________________ Decorate the can with glitter and stickers.

Sequencing: Making Clay

Directions: Read about making clay. Then, follow the instructions.

It is fun to work with clay. Here is what you need to make it:

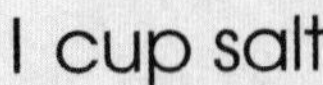

1 cup salt

2 cups flour

3/4 cup water

Mix the salt and flour. Then, add the water. Do not eat the clay. It tastes bad. Use your hands to mix and mix. Now, roll it out. What can you make with your clay?

1. Circle the main idea:

   Do not eat clay.

   Mix salt, flour, and water to make clay.

2. Write the steps for making clay.

   a. ____________________

   b. ____________________

   c. Mix the clay.

   d. ____________________

3. Write why you should not eat clay. ________________

Fact and Opinion: Recycling

Directions: Read about recycling. Then, follow the instructions.

What do you throw away every day? What could you do with these things? You could change an old greeting card into a new card. You could make a puppet with an old paper bag. Old buttons make great refrigerator magnets. You can plant seeds in plastic cups. Cardboard tubes make perfect rockets. So, use your imagination!

Write **F** next to each fact and **O** next to each opinion.

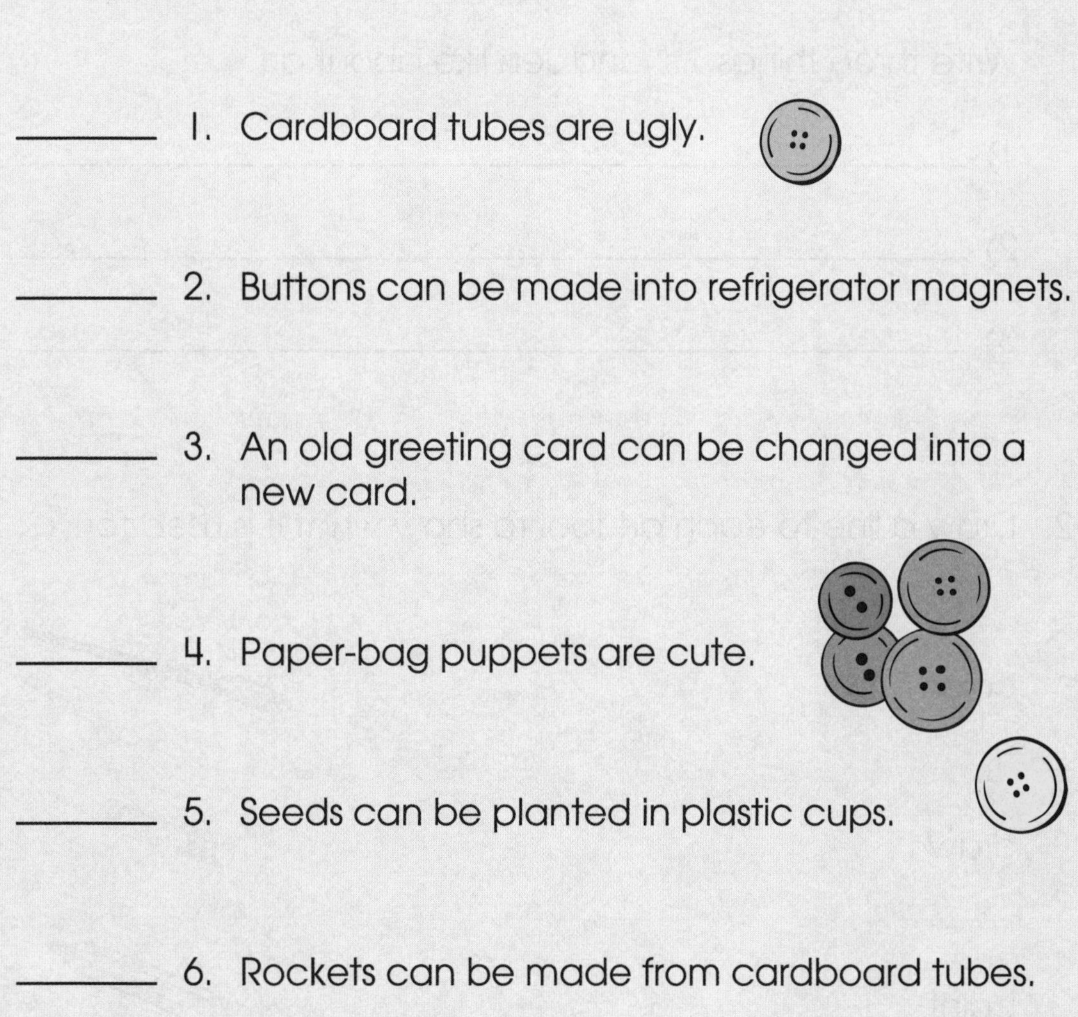

_______ 1. Cardboard tubes are ugly.

_______ 2. Buttons can be made into refrigerator magnets.

_______ 3. An old greeting card can be changed into a new card.

_______ 4. Paper-bag puppets are cute.

_______ 5. Seeds can be planted in plastic cups.

_______ 6. Rockets can be made from cardboard tubes.

Making Inferences: J.J. and Jen Like Art

Directions: Read about J.J. and Jen. Then, follow the instructions.

J.J. and Jen like art. They both like to draw and paint colorful pictures. They both like to make things from junk that they find at home. They like to use their hands to mold clay into different shapes. Do you like art?

1. Write three things J.J. and Jen like about art.

   1) ______________________________

   2) ______________________________

   3) ______________________________

2. Draw a line to each art tool to show what it is used for.

   color

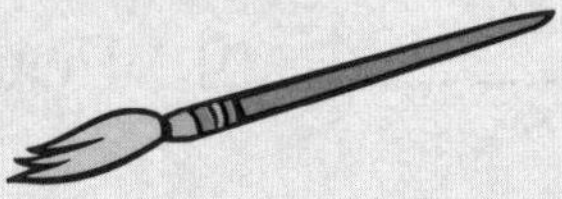

   draw

   paint

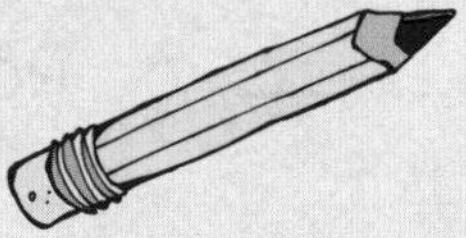

Fiction and Nonfiction: Which is It?

Directions: Read about fiction and nonfiction books. Then, follow the instructions.

There are many kinds of books. Some books have make-believe stories about princesses and dragons. Some books contain poetry and rhymes, like Mother Goose. These are fiction. Some books contain facts about space and plants. And still, other books have stories about famous people in history, like Abraham Lincoln. These are nonfiction.

Write **F** for fiction and **NF** for nonfiction.

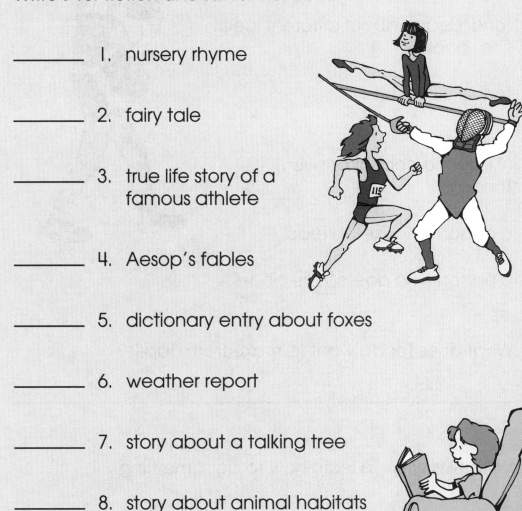

_______ 1. nursery rhyme

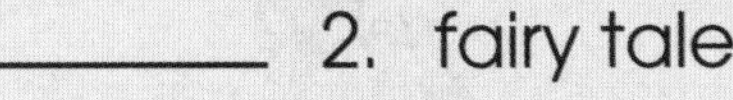

_______ 2. fairy tale

_______ 3. true life story of a famous athlete

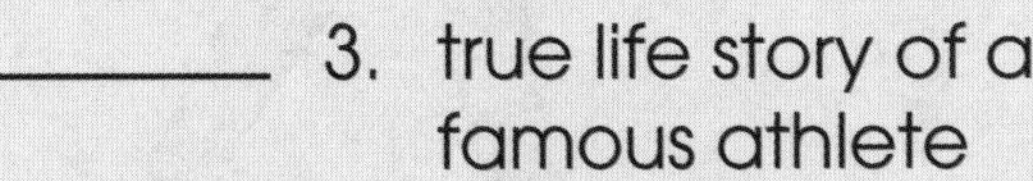

_______ 4. Aesop's fables

_______ 5. dictionary entry about foxes

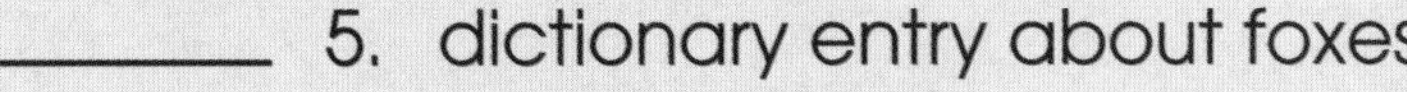

_______ 6. weather report

_______ 7. story about a talking tree

_______ 8. story about animal habitats

_______ 9. riddles and jokes

Comprehension: Ideas Come From Books

Directions: Read the story. Then, follow the instructions.

Tonda has many books. She gets different ideas from these books. Some of her books are about fish. Some are about cardboard and paper crafts. Some are about nature. Others are about reusing junk. Tonda wants to make a paper airplane. She reads about it in one of her books. Then, she asks an adult to help her.

1. Circle the main idea:

   Tonda learns about different ideas from books.

   Tonda likes crafts.

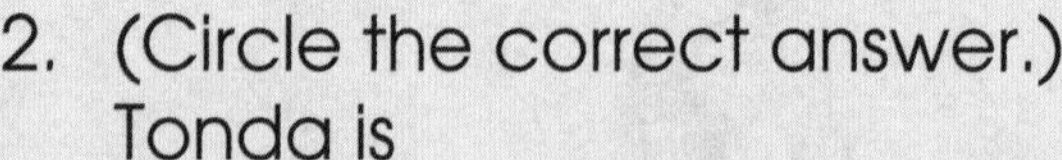

2. (Circle the correct answer.)
   Tonda is

   a person who likes to read.

   a person who doesn't like books.

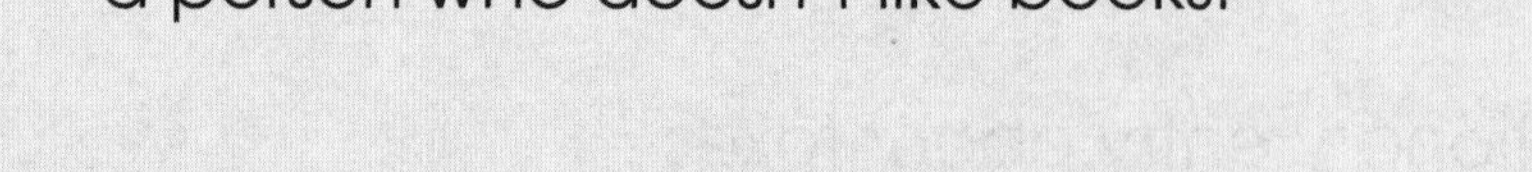

3. What does Tonda want to make from paper?

   ____

4. Write two ways to learn how to do something.

   1) ______________________________

   2) ______________________________

Review

Directions: Read the story. Then, answer the questions.

Randa, Emily, Ali, Dave, Liesl, and Deana all love to read. Every Tuesday, they all go to the library together and pick out their favorite books. Randa likes books about fish. Emily likes books about sports and athletes. Ali likes books about art. Dave likes books about wild animals. Liesl likes books with riddles and puzzles. Deanna likes books about cats and dogs.

1. Circle the main idea:

   Randa, Emily, Ali, Dave, Liesl, and Deana are good friends.

   Randa, Emily, Ali, Dave, Liesl, and Deana all like books.

2. Who do you think might grow up to be an artist?

   ____

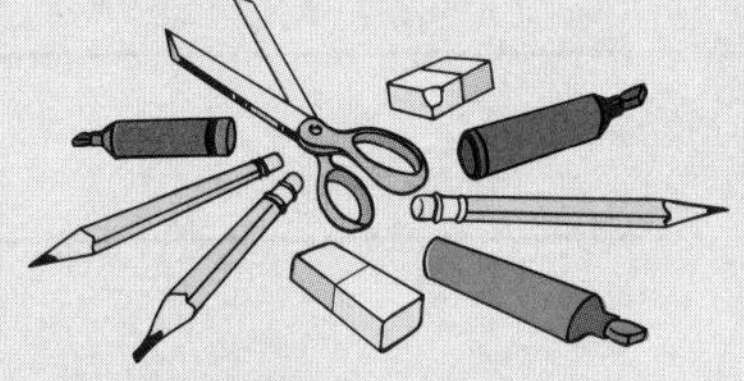

3. Who do you think might grow up to be an oceanographer (someone who studies the ocean)?

   ____

4. Who do you think might grow up to be a veterinarian (an animal doctor)?

   ____

All About You!

In this book, you learned about many children and what they like to do. You have many interests, too!

Directions: Write a story telling what you like to do. Then, draw a picture to go with your story on the next page.

Draw what you like to do.

Glossary

Classifying: Putting things that are alike into groups.

Comprehension: Understanding what you read.

Fact: Something that can be proven.

Fiction: A make-believe story.

Homophones: Words that sound alike, but have different spellings and meanings. **Example**: **read** and **red**.

Inference: A conclusion arrived at by what is suggested in the text.

Main Idea: The most important point or idea in a story.

Nonfiction: A true story.

Opinion: A feeling or belief about something that cannot be proven.

Predicting: Telling what is likely to happen based on the facts.

Prefix: A syllable added to the beginning of a word that changes its meaning.

Sequencing: Putting things in the correct order.

Venn Diagram: A diagram that shows how two things are the same and different.

Answer Key

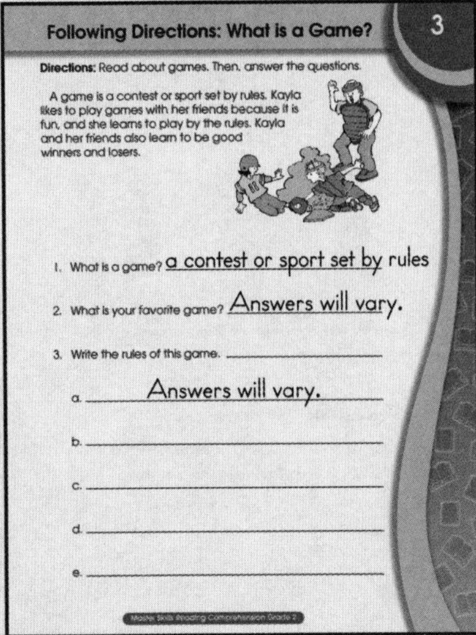

Following Directions: What is a Game? 3

Directions: Read about games. Then, answer the questions.

A game is a contest or sport set by rules. Kayla likes to play games with her friends because it is fun, and she learns to play by the rules. Kayla and her friends also learn to be good winners and losers.

1. What is a game? a contest or sport set by rules
2. What is your favorite game? Answers will vary.
3. Write the rules of this game.
   a. Answers will vary.
   b.
   c.
   d.
   e.

Master Skills Reading Comprehension Grade 2

3

4 Classifying: Outdoor/Indoor Games

Classifying is putting things that are alike into groups.

Directions: Read about games. Draw an **X** on the games you can play indoors. Circle the objects used for outdoor games.

Some games are outdoor games. Some games are indoor games. Outdoor games are active. Indoor games are quiet.

Which game do you like best? Answers will vary.

Master Skills Reading Comprehension Grade 2

4

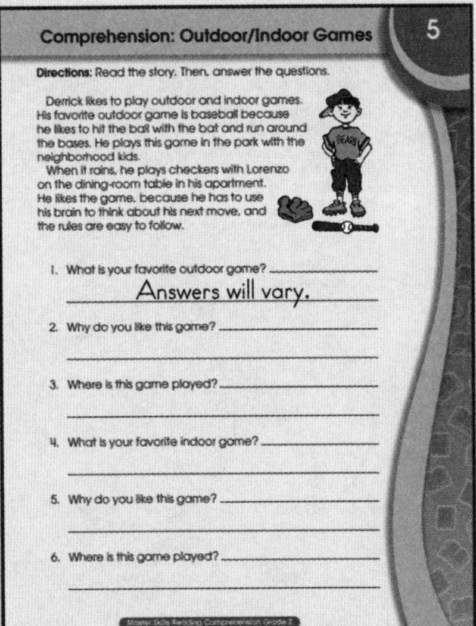

Comprehension: Outdoor/Indoor Games 5

Directions: Read the story. Then, answer the questions.

Derrick likes to play outdoor and indoor games. His favorite outdoor game is baseball because he likes to hit the ball with the bat and run around the bases. He plays this game in the park with the neighborhood kids.

When it rains, he plays checkers with Lorenzo on the dining-room table in his apartment. He likes the game, because he has to use his brain to think about his next move, and the rules are easy to follow.

1. What is your favorite outdoor game? Answers will vary.
2. Why do you like this game?
3. Where is this game played?
4. What is your favorite indoor game?
5. Why do you like this game?
6. Where is this game played?

Master Skills Reading Comprehension Grade 2

5

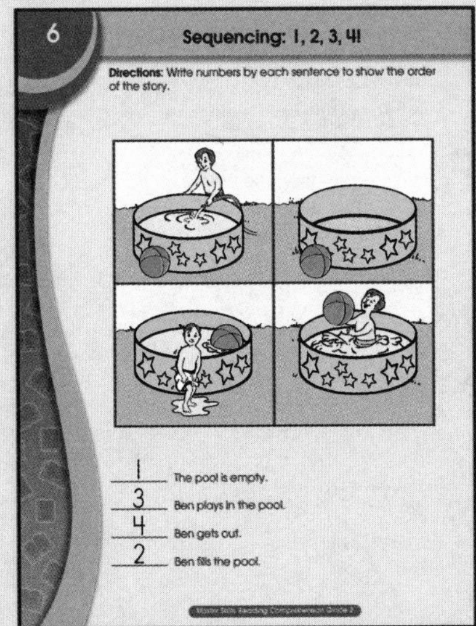

6 Sequencing: 1, 2, 3, 4!

Directions: Write numbers by each sentence to show the order of the story.

1 The pool is empty.
3 Ben plays in the pool.
4 Ben gets out.
2 Ben fills the pool.

Master Skills Reading Comprehension Grade 2

6

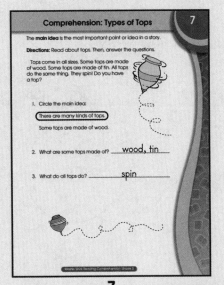

Comprehension: Types of Tops 7

The **main idea** is the most important point or idea in a story.

Directions: Read about tops. Then, answer the questions.

Tops come in all sizes. Some tops are made of wood. Some tops are made of tin. All tops do the same thing. They spin! Do you have a top?

1. Circle the main idea:
   (There are many kinds of tops.)
   Some tops are made of wood.
2. What are some tops made of? wood, tin
3. What do all tops do? spin

Master Skills Reading Comprehension Grade 2

7

8 Making Inferences: Ryan's Top

Directions: Read about Ryan's top. Then, follow the instructions.

Ryan got a new top. He wanted to place it where it would be safe. He asked his dad to put it up high. Where can his dad put the top?

Answers may include:

1. Write where Ryan's dad can put the top.
   on top of the refrigerator, on a closet shelf

Draw a place Ryan's dad can put the top.

Drawings will vary.

Master Skills Reading Comprehension Grade 2

8

Answer Key

Comprehension: Yo-Yos 9

Directions: Read about yo-yos. Then, follow the instructions.

Yo-yo is a funny word. It means "come-come." Why? Move the yo-yo away from you on its string. It will come back!

1. Circle the main idea:

You can move a yo-yo on a string.

Yo-yo means "come-come" because it always comes back.

2. (Circle the correct answer.) A yo-yo moves:

slowly

on a string

3. Color the yo-yo.

Master Skills Reading Comprehension Grade 2

9

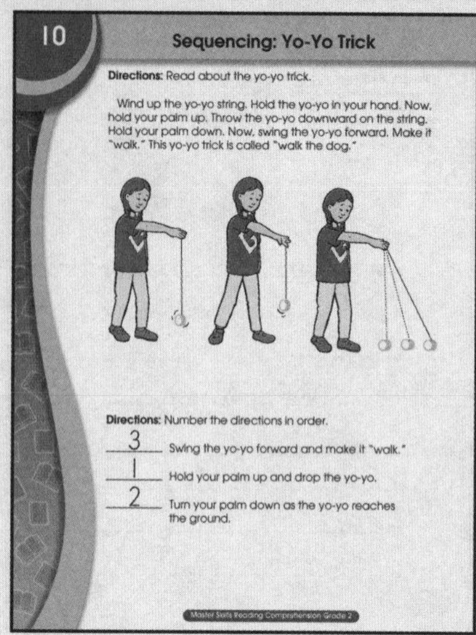

10 Sequencing: Yo-Yo Trick

Directions: Read about the yo-yo trick.

Wind up the yo-yo string. Hold the yo-yo in your hand. Now, hold your palm up. Throw the yo-yo downward on the string. Hold your palm down. Now, swing the yo-yo forward. Make it "walk." This yo-yo trick is called "walk the dog."

Directions: Number the directions in order.

3 Swing the yo-yo forward and make it "walk."

1 Hold your palm up and drop the yo-yo.

2 Turn your palm down as the yo-yo reaches the ground.

Master Skills Reading Comprehension Grade 2

10

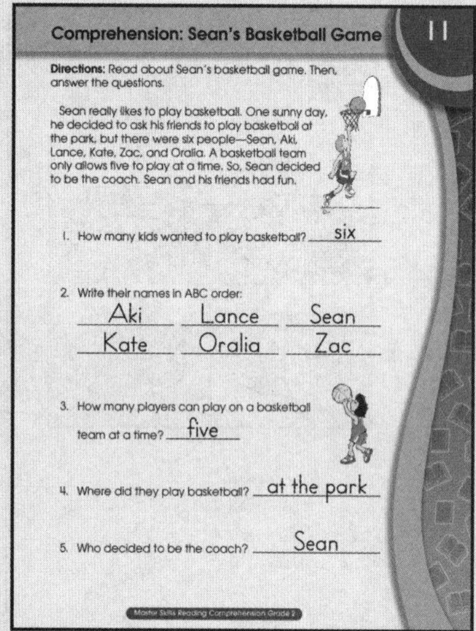

Comprehension: Sean's Basketball Game 11

Directions: Read about Sean's basketball game. Then, answer the questions.

Sean really likes to play basketball. One sunny day, he decided to ask his friends to play basketball at the park, but there were six people—Sean, Aki, Lance, Kate, Zac, and Oralia. A basketball team only allows five to play at a time. So, Sean decided to be the coach. Sean and his friends had fun.

1. How many kids wanted to play basketball? six

2. Write their names in ABC order:

Aki Lance Sean
Kate Oralia Zac

3. How many players can play on a basketball team at a time? five

4. Where did they play basketball? at the park

5. Who decided to be the coach? Sean

Master Skills Reading Comprehension Grade 2

11

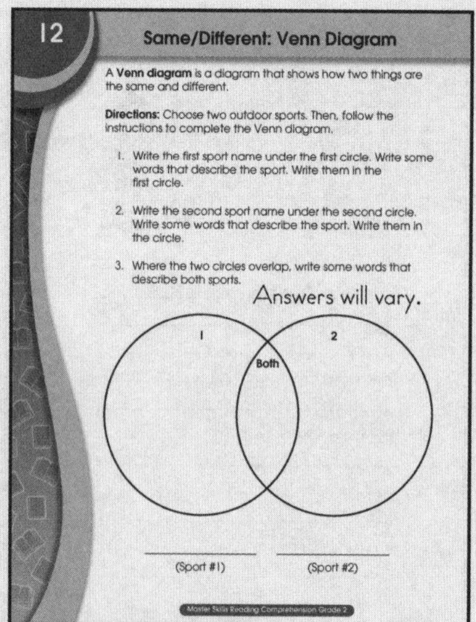

12 Same/Different: Venn Diagram

A **Venn diagram** is a diagram that shows how two things are the same and different.

Directions: Choose two outdoor sports. Then, follow the instructions to complete the Venn diagram.

1. Write the first sport name under the first circle. Write some words that describe the sport. Write them in the first circle.
2. Write the second sport name under the second circle. Write some words that describe the sport. Write them in the circle.
3. Where the two circles overlap, write some words that describe both sports.

Answers will vary.

1 Both 2

(Sport #1) (Sport #2)

Master Skills Reading Comprehension Grade 2

12

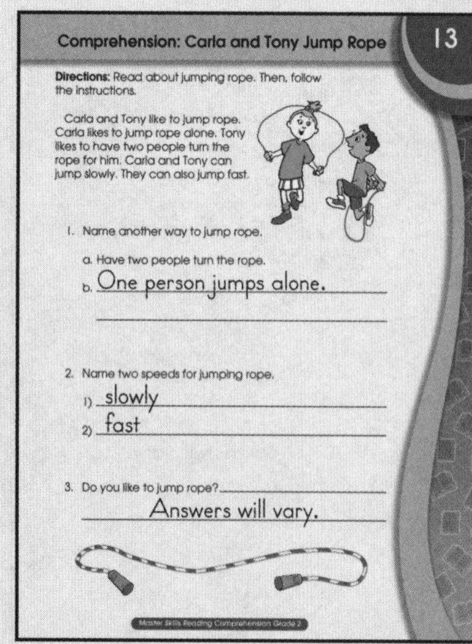

Comprehension: Carla and Tony Jump Rope 13

Directions: Read about jumping rope. Then, follow the instructions.

Carla and Tony like to jump rope. Carla likes to jump rope alone. Tony likes to have two people turn the rope for him. Carla and Tony can jump slowly. They can also jump fast.

1. Name another way to jump rope.

a. Have two people turn the rope.

b. One person jumps alone.

2. Name two speeds for jumping rope.

1) slowly

2) fast

3. Do you like to jump rope?

Answers will vary.

Master Skills Reading Comprehension Grade 2

13

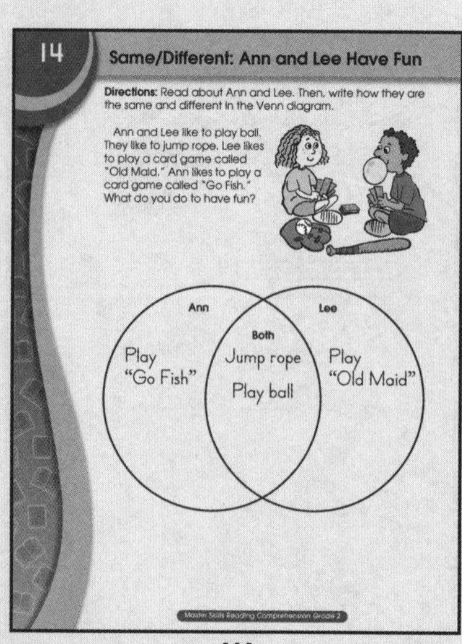

14 Same/Different: Ann and Lee Have Fun

Directions: Read about Ann and Lee. Then, write how they are the same and different in the Venn diagram.

Ann and Lee like to play ball. They like to jump rope. Lee likes to play a card game called "Old Maid." Ann likes to play a card game called "Go Fish." What do you do to have fun?

Ann: Play "Go Fish"

Both: Jump rope, Play ball

Lee: Play "Old Maid"

Master Skills Reading Comprehension Grade 2

14

Answer Key

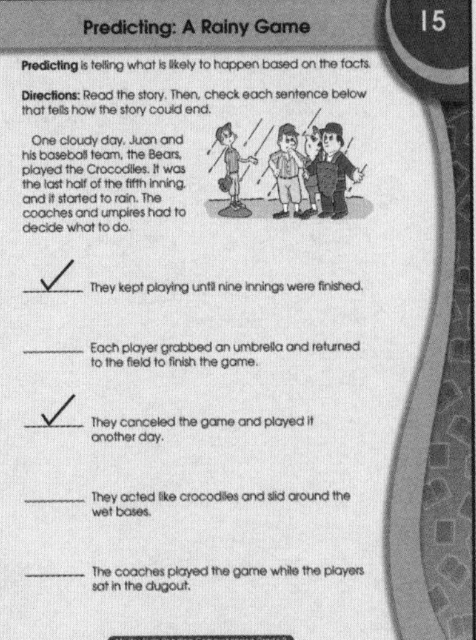

15 Predicting: A Rainy Game

Predicting is telling what is likely to happen based on the facts.

Directions: Read the story. Then, check each sentence below that tells how the story could end.

One cloudy day, Juan and his baseball team, the Bears, played the Crocodiles. It was the last half of the fifth inning, and it started to rain. The coaches and umpires had to decide what to do.

✓ They kept playing until nine innings were finished.

_____ Each player grabbed an umbrella and returned to the field to finish the game.

✓ They canceled the game and played it another day.

_____ They acted like crocodiles and slid around the wet bases.

_____ The coaches played the game while the players sat in the dugout.

Master Skills Reading Comprehension Grade 2

15

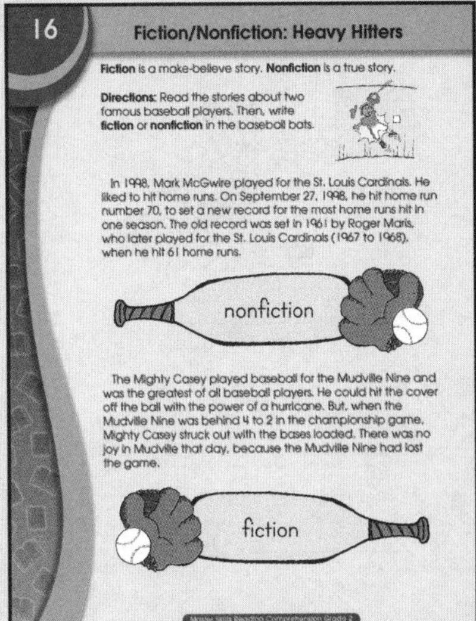

16 Fiction/Nonfiction: Heavy Hitters

Fiction is a make-believe story. **Nonfiction** is a true story.

Directions: Read the stories about two famous baseball players. Then, write **fiction** or **nonfiction** in the baseball bats.

In 1998, Mark McGwire played for the St. Louis Cardinals. He liked to hit home runs. On September 27, 1998, he hit home run number 70, to set a new record for the most home runs hit in one season. The old record was set in 1961 by Roger Maris, who later played for the St. Louis Cardinals (1967 to 1968), when he hit 61 home runs.

nonfiction

The Mighty Casey played baseball for the Mudville Nine and was the greatest of all baseball players. He could hit the cover off the ball with the power of a hurricane. But, when the Mudville Nine was behind 4 to 2 in the championship game, Mighty Casey struck out with the bases loaded. There was no joy in Mudville that day, because the Mudville Nine had lost the game.

fiction

Master Skills Reading Comprehension Grade 2

16

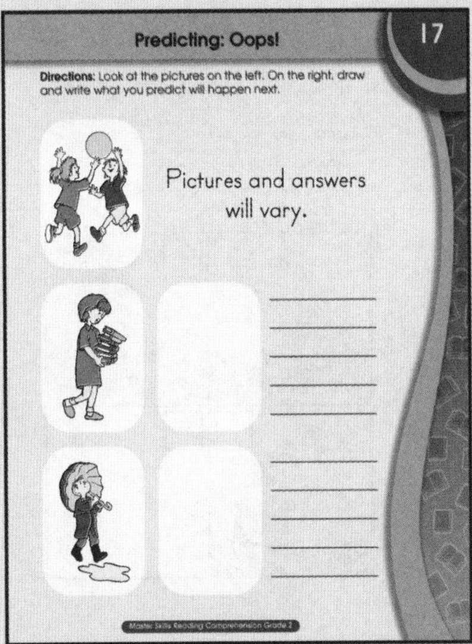

17 Predicting: Oops!

Directions: Look at the pictures on the left. On the right, draw and write what you predict will happen next.

Pictures and answers will vary.

Master Skills Reading Comprehension Grade 2

17

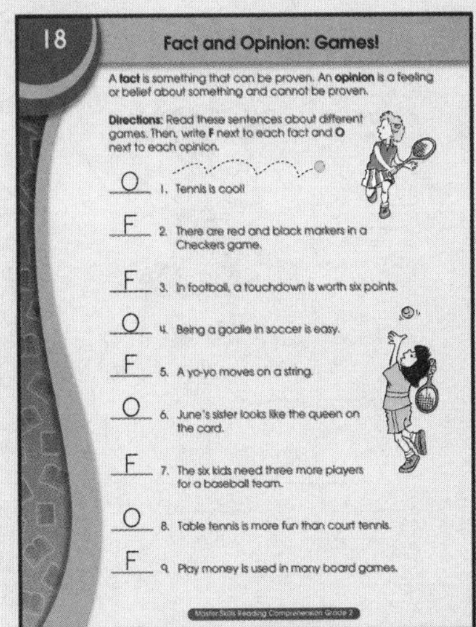

18 Fact and Opinion: Games!

A **fact** is something that can be proven. An **opinion** is a feeling or belief about something and cannot be proven.

Directions: Read these sentences about different games. Then, write **F** next to each fact and **O** next to each opinion.

O 1. Tennis is cool!

F 2. There are red and black markers in a Checkers game.

F 3. In football, a touchdown is worth six points.

O 4. Being a goalie in soccer is easy.

F 5. A yo-yo moves on a string.

O 6. June's sister looks like the queen on the card.

F 7. The six kids need three more players for a baseball team.

O 8. Table tennis is more fun than court tennis.

F 9. Play money is used in many board games.

Master Skills Reading Comprehension Grade 2

18

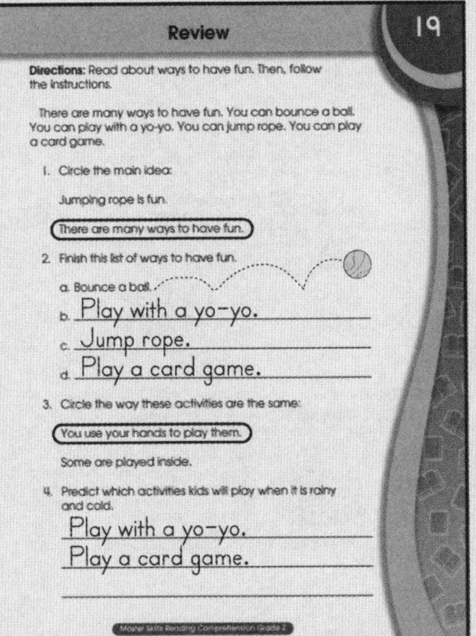

19 Review

Directions: Read about ways to have fun. Then, follow the instructions.

There are many ways to have fun. You can bounce a ball. You can play with a yo-yo. You can jump rope. You can play a card game.

1. Circle the main idea:

   Jumping rope is fun.

   (There are many ways to have fun.)

2. Finish this list of ways to have fun.

   a. Bounce a ball.
   b. Play with a yo-yo.
   c. Jump rope.
   d. Play a card game.

3. Circle the way these activities are the same:

   (You use your hands to play them.)

   Some are played inside.

4. Predict which activities kids will play when it is rainy and cold.

   Play with a yo-yo.
   Play a card game.

Master Skills Reading Comprehension Grade 2

19

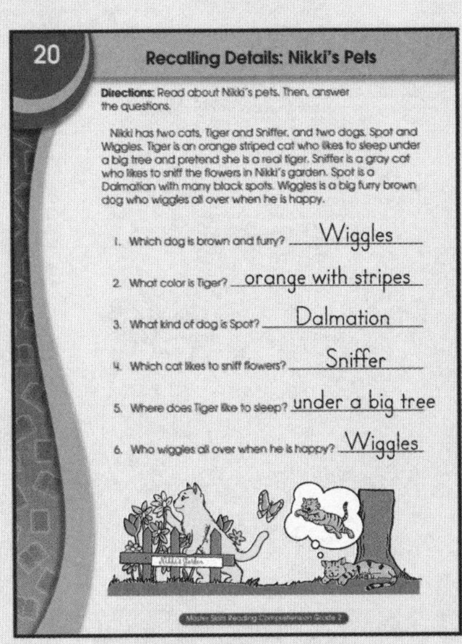

20 Recalling Details: Nikki's Pets

Directions: Read about Nikki's pets. Then, answer the questions.

Nikki has two cats, Tiger and Sniffer, and two dogs, Spot and Wiggles. Tiger is an orange striped cat who likes to sleep under a big tree and pretend she is a real tiger. Sniffer is a gray cat who likes to sniff the flowers in Nikki's garden. Spot is a Dalmatian with many black spots. Wiggles is a big furry brown dog who wiggles all over when he is happy.

1. Which dog is brown and furry? Wiggles
2. What color is Tiger? orange with stripes
3. What kind of dog is Spot? Dalmation
4. Which cat likes to sniff flowers? Sniffer
5. Where does Tiger like to sleep? under a big tree
6. Who wiggles all over when he is happy? Wiggles

Master Skills Reading Comprehension Grade 2

20

Answer Key

Predicting: KD Likes Milk

21

Directions: Read about KD the cat. Then, write what you think she will do.

KD likes milk. Perla, KD's owner, set out a pan of juice. Then, she set out a pan of milk.

1. What will KD do? Answers will vary.
2. Why?

Master Skills Reading Comprehension Grade 2

21

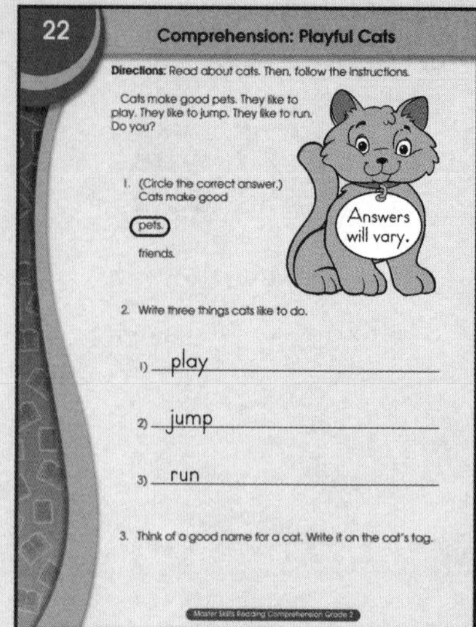

Comprehension: Playful Cats

22

Directions: Read about cats. Then, follow the instructions.

Cats make good pets. They like to play. They like to jump. They like to run. Do you?

1. (Circle the correct answer.) Cats make good
   (pets.)
   friends.
2. Write three things cats like to do.
   1) play
   2) jump
   3) run
3. Think of a good name for a cat. Write it on the cat's tag.

Answers will vary.

Master Skills Reading Comprehension Grade 2

22

Predicting: What Will Bobby Do?

23

Directions: Read about Bobby the cat. Then, write what you think will happen.

One sunny spring day, Bobby was sleeping under her favorite tree. She was dreaming about her favorite food—tuna. Suddenly, she became hungry for a treat. Bobby woke up and listened when she heard someone call her name.

1. Why do you think Bobby was being called? Answers will vary.
2. What do you think will happen next?

Master Skills Reading Comprehension Grade 2

23

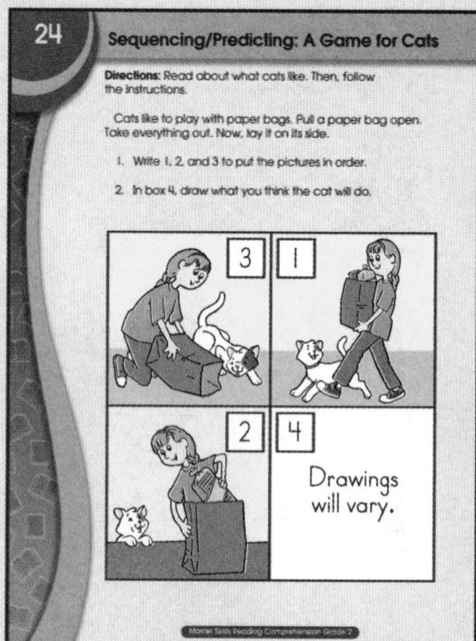

Sequencing/Predicting: A Game for Cats

24

Directions: Read about what cats like. Then, follow the instructions.

Cats like to play with paper bags. Pull a paper bag open. Take everything out. Now, lay it on its side.

1. Write 1, 2, and 3 to put the pictures in order.
2. In box 4, draw what you think the cat will do.

3 | 1 | 2 | 4

Drawings will vary.

Master Skills Reading Comprehension Grade 2

24

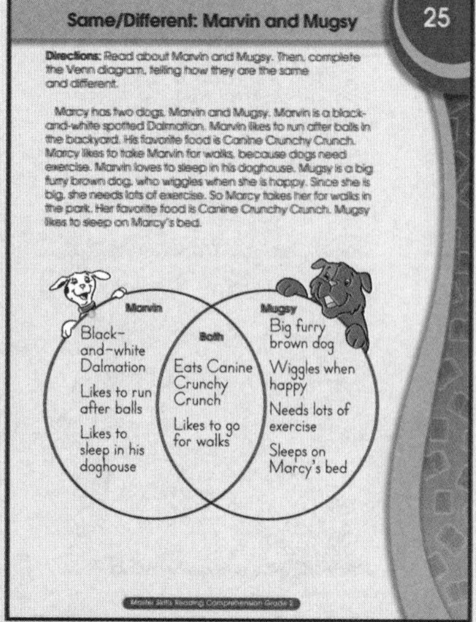

Same/Different: Marvin and Mugsy

25

Directions: Read about Marvin and Mugsy. Then, complete the Venn diagram, telling how they are the same and different.

Marcy has two dogs, Marvin and Mugsy. Marvin is a black-and-white spotted Dalmatian. Marvin likes to run after balls in the backyard. His favorite food is Canine Crunchy Crunch. Marcy likes to take Marvin for walks, because dogs need exercise. Marvin loves to sleep in his doghouse. Mugsy is a big furry brown dog, who wiggles when she is happy. Since she is big, she needs lots of exercise. So Marcy takes her for walks in the park. Her favorite food is Canine Crunchy Crunch. Mugsy likes to sleep on Marcy's bed.

Master Skills Reading Comprehension Grade 2

25

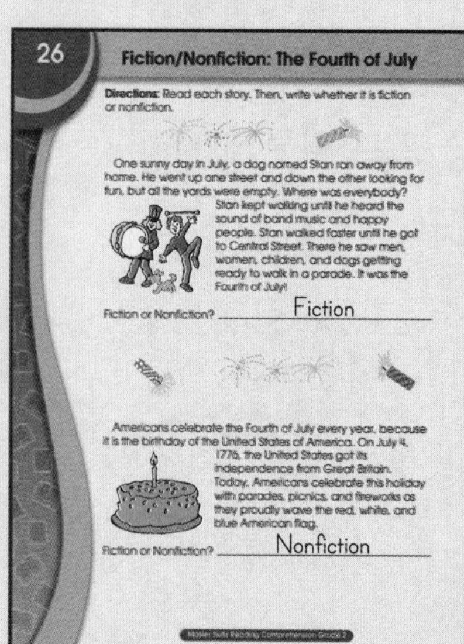

Fiction/Nonfiction: The Fourth of July

26

Directions: Read each story. Then, write whether it is fiction or nonfiction.

One sunny day in July, a dog named Stan ran away from home. He went up one street and down the other looking for fun, but all the yards were empty. Where was everybody? Stan kept walking until he heard the sound of band music and happy people. Stan walked faster until he got to Central Street. There he saw men, women, children, and dogs getting ready to walk in a parade. It was the Fourth of July!

Fiction or Nonfiction? Fiction

Americans celebrate the Fourth of July every year, because it is the birthday of the United States of America. On July 4, 1776, the United States got its independence from Great Britain. Today, Americans celebrate this holiday with parades, picnics, and fireworks as they proudly wave the red, white, and blue American flag.

Fiction or Nonfiction? Nonfiction

Master Skills Reading Comprehension Grade 2

26

Answer Key

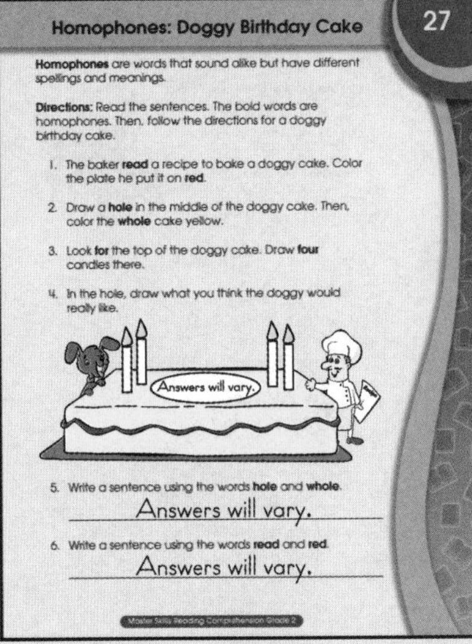
Homophones: Doggy Birthday Cake 27

Homophones are words that sound alike but have different spellings and meanings.

Directions: Read the sentences. The bold words are homophones. Then, follow the directions for a doggy birthday cake.

1. The baker **read** a recipe to bake a doggy cake. Color the plate he put it on **red**.
2. Draw a **hole** in the middle of the doggy cake. Then, color the **whole** cake yellow.
3. Look **for** the top of the doggy cake. Draw **four** candles there.
4. In the hole, draw what you think the doggy would really like.

Answers will vary.

5. Write a sentence using the words **hole** and **whole**.
Answers will vary.
6. Write a sentence using the words **read** and **red**.
Answers will vary.

Master Skills Reading Comprehension Grade 2

27

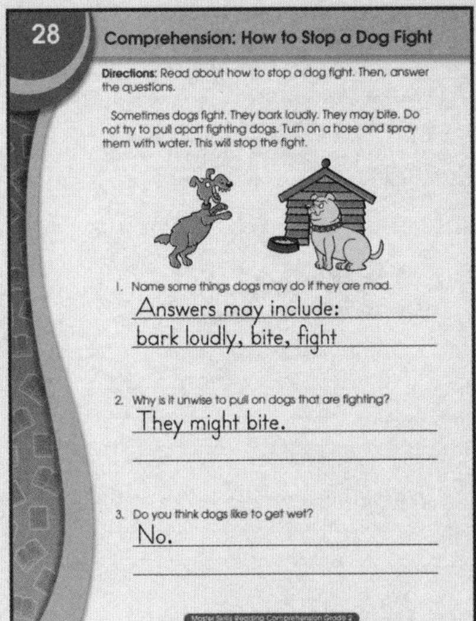
28 Comprehension: How to Stop a Dog Fight

Directions: Read about how to stop a dog fight. Then, answer the questions.

Sometimes dogs fight. They bark loudly. They may bite. Do not try to pull apart fighting dogs. Turn on a hose and spray them with water. This will stop the fight.

1. Name some things dogs may do if they are mad.
Answers may include: bark loudly, bite, fight
2. Why is it unwise to pull on dogs that are fighting?
They might bite.
3. Do you think dogs like to get wet?
No.

Master Skills Reading Comprehension Grade 2

28

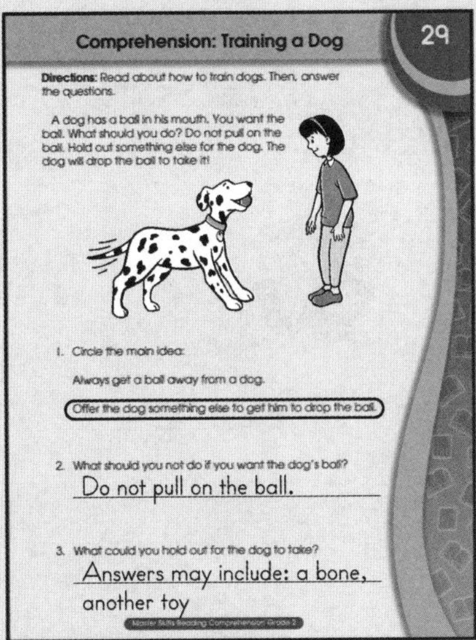
Comprehension: Training a Dog 29

Directions: Read about how to train dogs. Then, answer the questions.

A dog has a ball in his mouth. You want the ball. What should you do? Do not pull on the ball. Hold out something else for the dog. The dog will drop the ball to take it!

1. Circle the main idea:
Always get a ball away from a dog.
(Offer the dog something else to get him to drop the ball.)
2. What should you not do if you want the dog's ball?
Do not pull on the ball.
3. What could you hold out for the dog to take?
Answers may include: a bone, another toy

Master Skills Reading Comprehension Grade 2

29

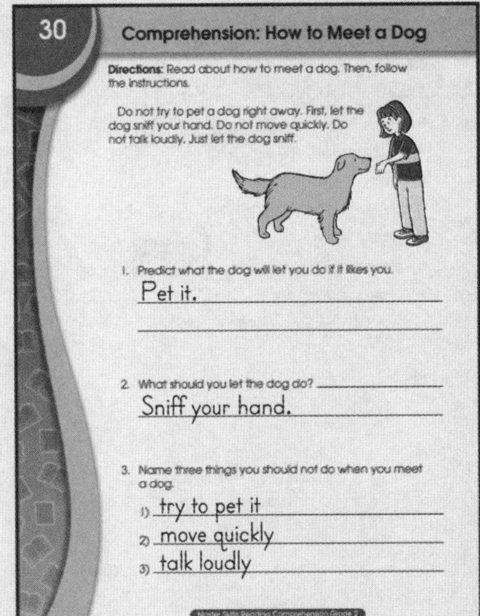
30 Comprehension: How to Meet a Dog

Directions: Read about how to meet a dog. Then, follow the instructions.

Do not try to pet a dog right away. First, let the dog sniff your hand. Do not move quickly. Do not talk loudly. Just let the dog sniff.

1. Predict what the dog will let you do if it likes you.
Pet it.
2. What should you let the dog do?
Sniff your hand.
3. Name three things you should not do when you meet a dog.
1) try to pet it
2) move quickly
3) talk loudly

Master Skills Reading Comprehension Grade 2

30

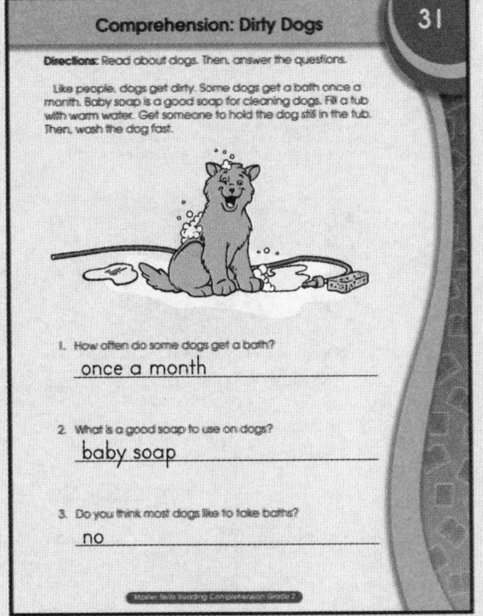
Comprehension: Dirty Dogs 31

Directions: Read about dogs. Then, answer the questions.

Like people, dogs get dirty. Some dogs get a bath once a month. Baby soap is a good soap for cleaning dogs. Fill a tub with warm water. Get someone to hold the dog still in the tub. Then, wash the dog fast.

1. How often do some dogs get a bath?
once a month
2. What is a good soap to use on dogs?
baby soap
3. Do you think most dogs like to take baths?
no

Master Skills Reading Comprehension Grade 2

31

32 Predicting: Dog-Gone!

Directions: Read the story. Then, follow the instructions.

Scotty and Simone were washing their dog, Willis. His fur was wet. Their hands were wet. Willis did not like to be wet. Scotty dropped the soap. Simone picked it up and let go of Willis. Uh-oh!

1. Write what happened next.
Answers will vary.
2. Draw what happened next.

Drawings will vary.

Master Skills Reading Comprehension Grade 2

32

Answer Key

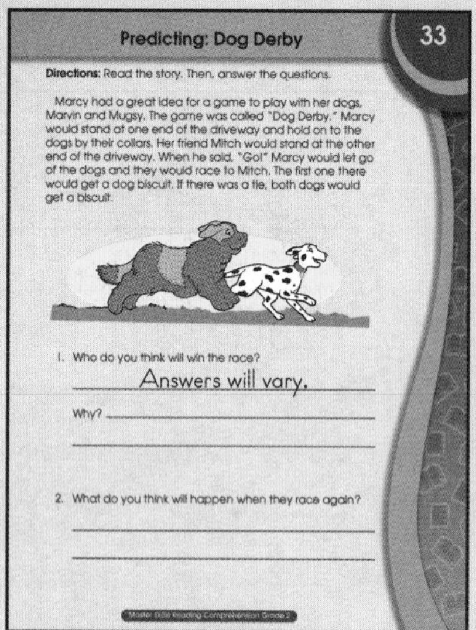

Predicting: Dog Derby 33

Directions: Read the story. Then, answer the questions.

Marcy had a great idea for a game to play with her dogs, Marvin and Mugsy. The game was called "Dog Derby." Marcy would stand at one end of the driveway and hold on to the dogs by their collars. Her friend Mitch would stand at the other end of the driveway. When he said, "Go!" Marcy would let go of the dogs and they would race to Mitch. The first one there would get a dog biscuit. If there was a tie, both dogs would get a biscuit.

1. Who do you think will win the race? Answers will vary.

   Why? _____

2. What do you think will happen when they race again? _____

Master Skills Reading Comprehension Grade 2

33

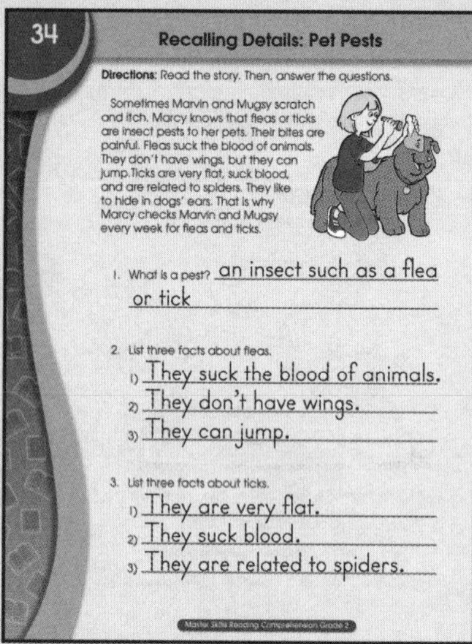

34 **Recalling Details: Pet Pests**

Directions: Read the story. Then, answer the questions.

Sometimes Marvin and Mugsy scratch and itch. Marcy knows that fleas or ticks are insect pests to her pets. Their bites are painful. Fleas suck the blood of animals. They don't have wings, but they can jump. Ticks are very flat, suck blood, and are related to spiders. They like to hide in dogs' ears. That is why Marcy checks Marvin and Mugsy every week for fleas and ticks.

1. What is a pest? an insect such as a flea or tick
2. List three facts about fleas.
   1) They suck the blood of animals.
   2) They don't have wings.
   3) They can jump.
3. List three facts about ticks.
   1) They are very flat.
   2) They suck blood.
   3) They are related to spiders.

Master Skills Reading Comprehension Grade 2

34

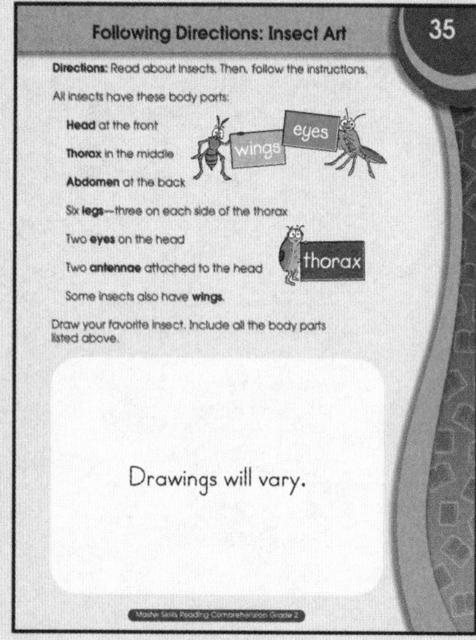

Following Directions: Insect Art 35

Directions: Read about insects. Then, follow the instructions.

All insects have these body parts:

Head at the front

Thorax in the middle

Abdomen at the back

Six **legs**—three on each side of the thorax

Two **eyes** on the head

Two **antennae** attached to the head

Some insects also have **wings**.

Draw your favorite insect. Include all the body parts listed above.

Drawings will vary.

Master Skills Reading Comprehension Grade 2

35

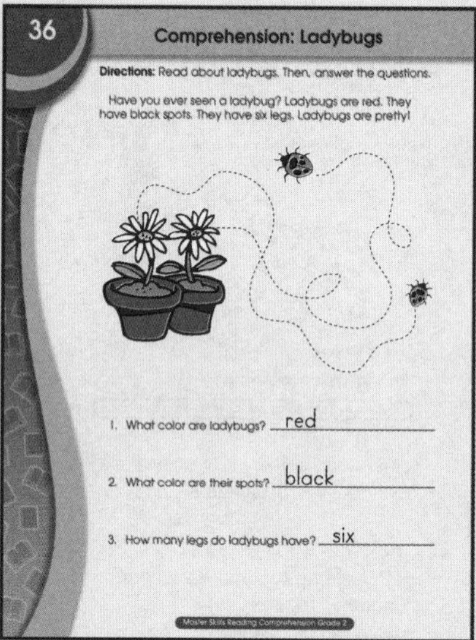

36 **Comprehension: Ladybugs**

Directions: Read about ladybugs. Then, answer the questions.

Have you ever seen a ladybug? Ladybugs are red. They have black spots. They have six legs. Ladybugs are pretty!

1. What color are ladybugs? red
2. What color are their spots? black
3. How many legs do ladybugs have? six

Master Skills Reading Comprehension Grade 2

36

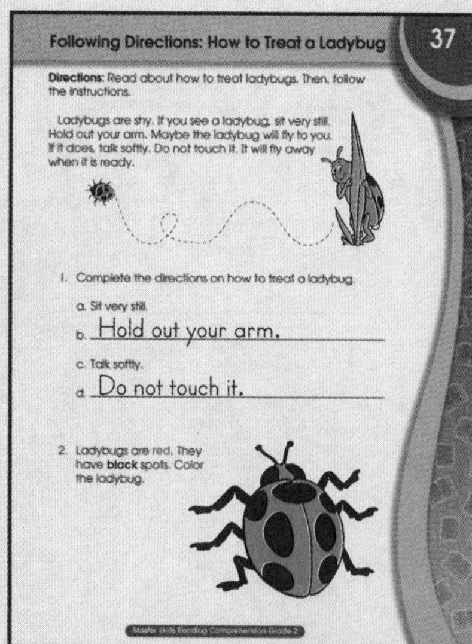

Following Directions: How to Treat a Ladybug 37

Directions: Read about how to treat ladybugs. Then, follow the instructions.

Ladybugs are shy. If you see a ladybug, sit very still. Hold out your arm. Maybe the ladybug will fly to you. If it does, talk softly. Do not touch it. It will fly away when it is ready.

1. Complete the directions on how to treat a ladybug.
   a. Sit very still.
   b. Hold out your arm.
   c. Talk softly.
   d. Do not touch it.
2. Ladybugs are red. They have **black** spots. Color the ladybug.

Master Skills Reading Comprehension Grade 2

37

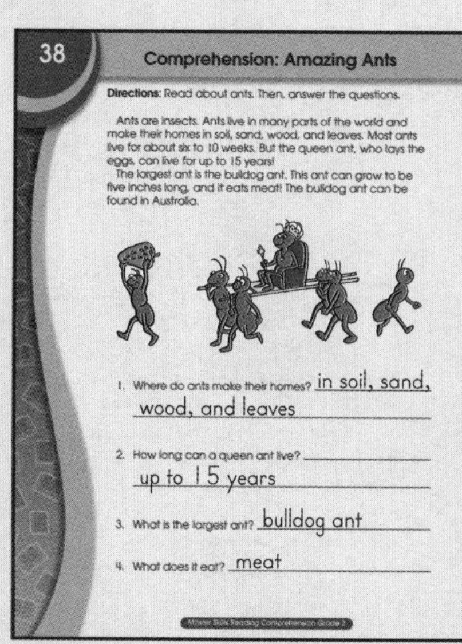

38 **Comprehension: Amazing Ants**

Directions: Read about ants. Then, answer the questions.

Ants are insects. Ants live in many parts of the world and make their homes in soil, sand, wood, and leaves. Most ants live for about six to 10 weeks. But the queen ant, who lays the eggs, can live for up to 15 years!

The largest ant is the bulldog ant. This ant can grow to be five inches long, and it eats meat! The bulldog ant can be found in Australia.

1. Where do ants make their homes? in soil, sand, wood, and leaves
2. How long can a queen ant live? up to 15 years
3. What is the largest ant? bulldog ant
4. What does it eat? meat

Master Skills Reading Comprehension Grade 2

38

Answer Key

Comprehension: Ant Farms 39

Directions: Read about ant farms. Then, answer the questions.

Ant farms are sold at toy stores and pet stores. Ant farms come in a flat frame. The frame has glass on each side. Inside the glass is sand. The ants live in the sand.

1. Where are ant farms sold? at toy stores and pet stores
2. The frame has glass on each side.
3. (Circle the correct answer.) The ants live in
   water. (sand.)
4. The ant farm frame is
   (flat.) round.

Master Skills Reading Comprehension Grade 2

39

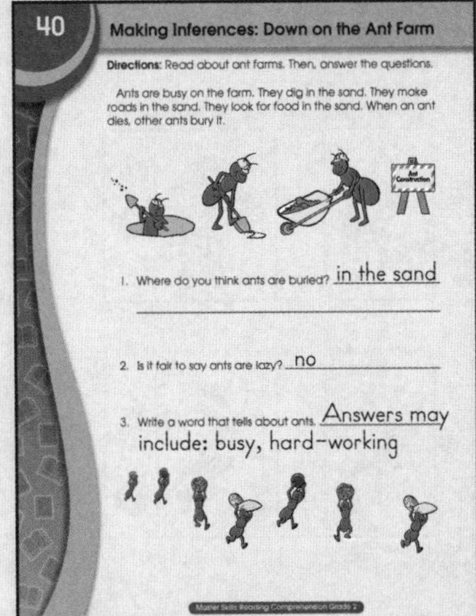

40 Making Inferences: Down on the Ant Farm

Directions: Read about ant farms. Then, answer the questions.

Ants are busy on the farm. They dig in the sand. They make roads in the sand. They look for food in the sand. When an ant dies, other ants bury it.

1. Where do you think ants are buried? in the sand
2. Is it fair to say ants are lazy? no
3. Write a word that tells about ants. Answers may include: busy, hard-working

Master Skills Reading Comprehension Grade 2

40

Review 41

Directions: Read about goats. Then, answer the questions.

Goats make good pets. Like cows, goats give milk. Cows eat grass. Goats eat grass, too.

Here is how to make a goat your pet: Three days after it is born, take it from its mother. Then, feed it from a bottle. Hold it and pet it. The goat will think you are its mother.

1. What do both goats and cows eat? grass
2. Circle the main idea:
   (Goats make good pets.)
   Goats and cows eat grass.
3. Tell how to make a pet of your goat.
   a. Take it from its mother when it is three days old.
   b. Feed it from a bottle.
   c. Hold it and pet it.
4. Why do you think the goat will think you are its mother?
   Because it gets its food from you just like it did from its mother.

Master Skills Reading Comprehension Grade 2

41

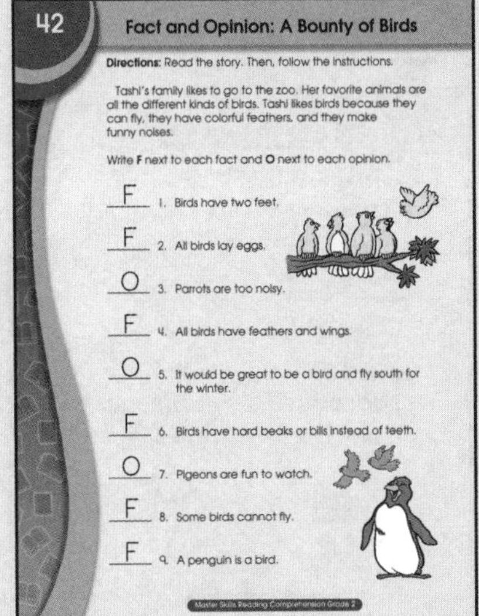

42 Fact and Opinion: A Bounty of Birds

Directions: Read the story. Then, follow the instructions.

Tashi's family likes to go to the zoo. Her favorite animals are all the different kinds of birds. Tashi likes birds because they can fly, they have colorful feathers, and they make funny noises.

Write **F** next to each fact and **O** next to each opinion.

F 1. Birds have two feet.
F 2. All birds lay eggs.
O 3. Parrots are too noisy.
F 4. All birds have feathers and wings.
O 5. It would be great to be a bird and fly south for the winter.
F 6. Birds have hard beaks or bills instead of teeth.
O 7. Pigeons are fun to watch.
F 8. Some birds cannot fly.
F 9. A penguin is a bird.

Master Skills Reading Comprehension Grade 2

42

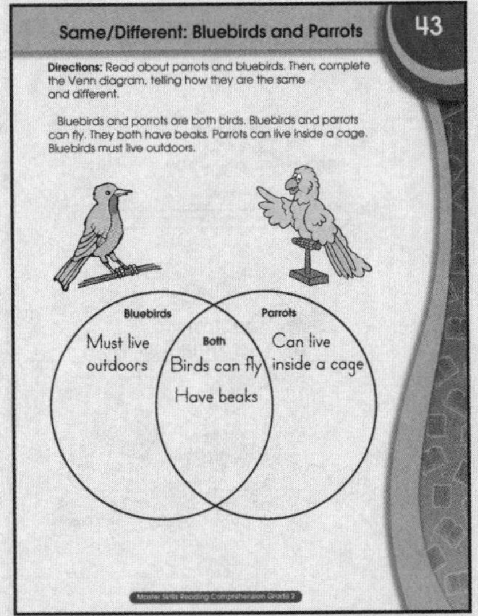

Same/Different: Bluebirds and Parrots 43

Directions: Read about parrots and bluebirds. Then, complete the Venn diagram, telling how they are the same and different.

Bluebirds and parrots are both birds. Bluebirds and parrots can fly. They both have beaks. Parrots can live inside a cage. Bluebirds must live outdoors.

Bluebirds	Both	Parrots
Must live outdoors	Birds can fly Have beaks	Can live inside a cage

Master Skills Reading Comprehension Grade 2

43

44 Comprehension: Pretty Parrots

Directions: Read about parrots. Then, follow the instructions.

Big parrots are pretty. Their feet have four toes each. Two toes are in front. Two toes are in back. Parrots use their feet to climb. They use them to hold food.

1. (Circle the correct answer.) A parrot's foot has
   (four toes.)
   two toes.
2. Name two things a parrot does with its feet.
   1) climb
   2) hold food
3. Color the parrot.

Master Skills Reading Comprehension Grade 2

44

Answer Key

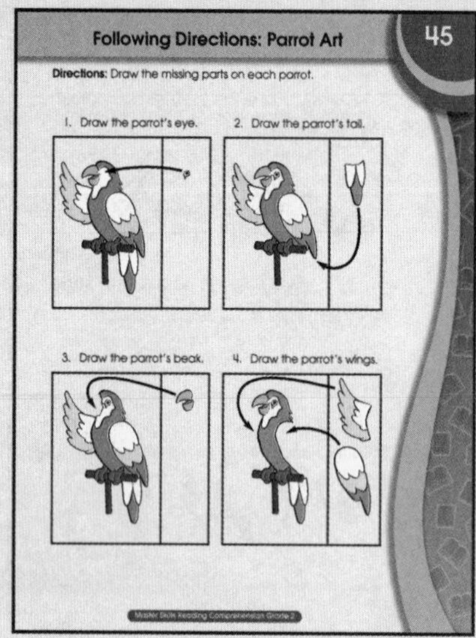

Following Directions: Parrot Art 45

Directions: Draw the missing parts on each parrot.

1. Draw the parrot's eye.
2. Draw the parrot's tail.
3. Draw the parrot's beak.
4. Draw the parrot's wings.

Master Skills Reading Comprehension Grade 2

45

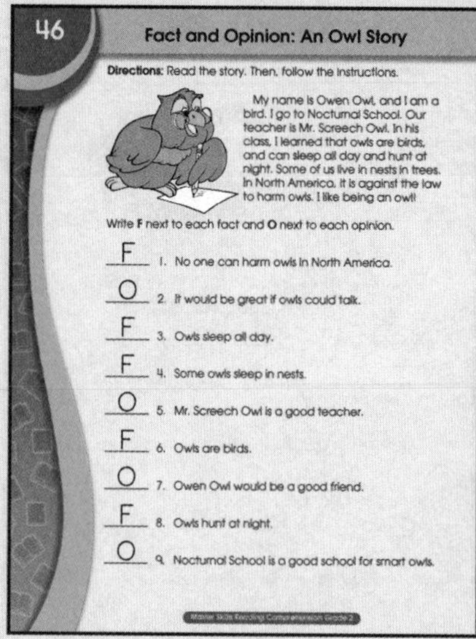

46 **Fact and Opinion: An Owl Story**

Directions: Read the story. Then, follow the instructions.

My name is Owen Owl, and I am a bird. I go to Nocturnal School. Our teacher is Mr. Screech Owl. In his class, I learned that owls are birds, and can sleep all day and hunt at night. Some of us live in nests in trees. In North America, it is against the law to harm owls. I like being an owl!

Write **F** next to each fact and **O** next to each opinion.

F 1. No one can harm owls in North America.
O 2. It would be great if owls could talk.
F 3. Owls sleep all day.
F 4. Some owls sleep in nests.
O 5. Mr. Screech Owl is a good teacher.
F 6. Owls are birds.
O 7. Owen Owl would be a good friend.
F 8. Owls hunt at night.
O 9. Nocturnal School is a good school for smart owls.

Master Skills Reading Comprehension Grade 2

46

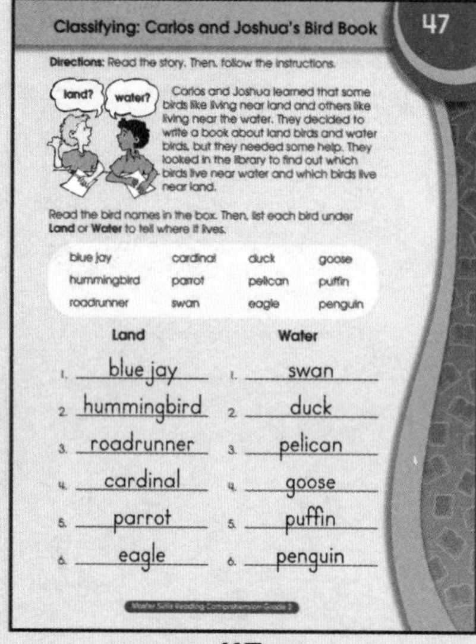

Classifying: Carlos and Joshua's Bird Book 47

Directions: Read the story. Then, follow the instructions.

Carlos and Joshua learned that some birds like living near land and others like living near the water. They decided to write a book about land birds and water birds, but they needed some help. They looked in the library to find out which birds live near water and which birds live near land.

Read the bird names in the box. Then, list each bird under **Land** or **Water** to tell where it lives.

blue jay	cardinal	duck	goose
hummingbird	parrot	pelican	puffin
roadrunner	swan	eagle	penguin

Land	Water
1. blue jay	1. swan
2. hummingbird	2. duck
3. roadrunner	3. pelican
4. cardinal	4. goose
5. parrot	5. puffin
6. eagle	6. penguin

Master Skills Reading Comprehension Grade 2

47

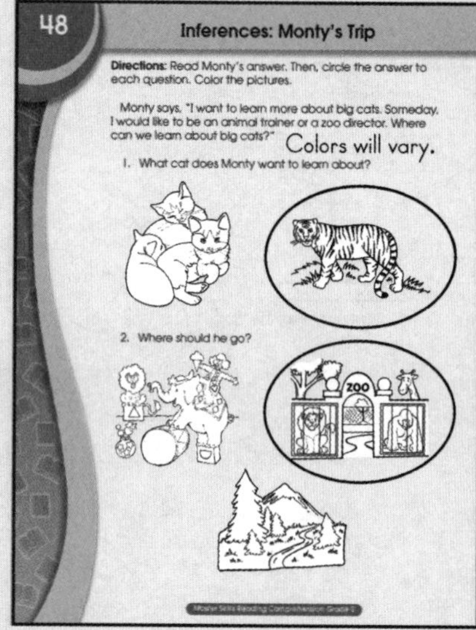

48 **Inferences: Monty's Trip**

Directions: Read Monty's answer. Then, circle the answer to each question. Color the pictures.

Monty says, "I want to learn more about big cats. Someday, I would like to be an animal trainer or a zoo director. Where can we learn about big cats?" Colors will vary.

1. What cat does Monty want to learn about?

2. Where should he go?

Master Skills Reading Comprehension Grade 2

48

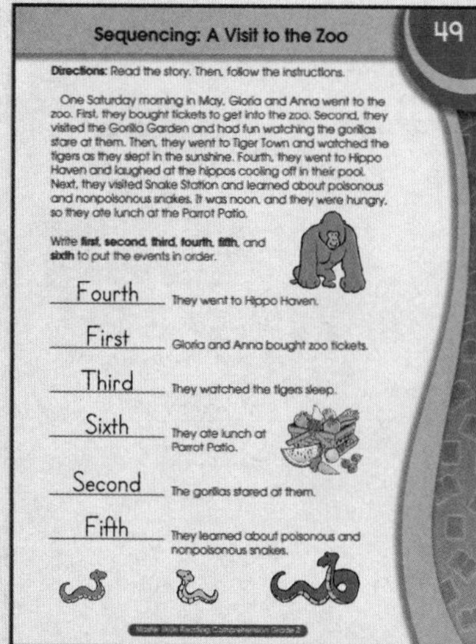

Sequencing: A Visit to the Zoo 49

Directions: Read the story. Then, follow the instructions.

One Saturday morning in May, Gloria and Anna went to the zoo. First, they bought tickets to get into the zoo. Second, they visited the Gorilla Garden and had fun watching the gorillas stare at them. Then, they went to Tiger Town and watched the tigers as they slept in the sunshine. Fourth, they went to Hippo Haven and laughed at the hippos cooling off in their pool. Next, they visited Snake Station and learned about poisonous and nonpoisonous snakes. It was noon, and they were hungry, so they ate lunch at the Parrot Patio.

Write **first**, **second**, **third**, **fourth**, **fifth**, and **sixth** to put the events in order.

Fourth They went to Hippo Haven.
First Gloria and Anna bought zoo tickets.
Third They watched the tigers sleep.
Sixth They ate lunch at Parrot Patio.
Second The gorillas stared at them.
Fifth They learned about poisonous and nonpoisonous snakes.

Master Skills Reading Comprehension Grade 2

49

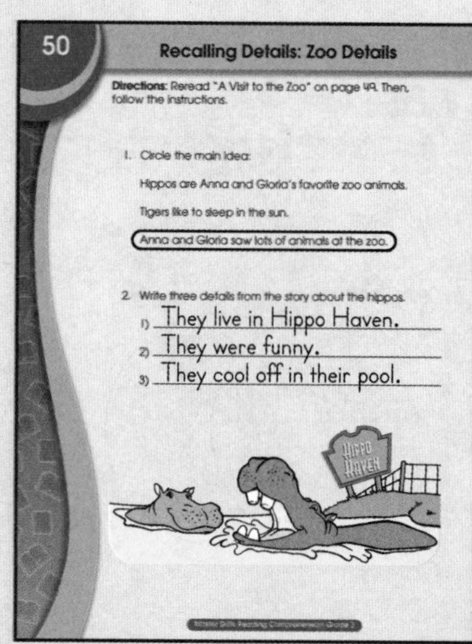

50 **Recalling Details: Zoo Details**

Directions: Reread "A Visit to the Zoo" on page 49. Then, follow the instructions.

1. Circle the main idea:

Hippos are Anna and Gloria's favorite zoo animals.

Tigers like to sleep in the sun.

(Anna and Gloria saw lots of animals at the zoo.)

2. Write three details from the story about the hippos.

1) They live in Hippo Haven.
2) They were funny.
3) They cool off in their pool.

Master Skills Reading Comprehension Grade 2

50

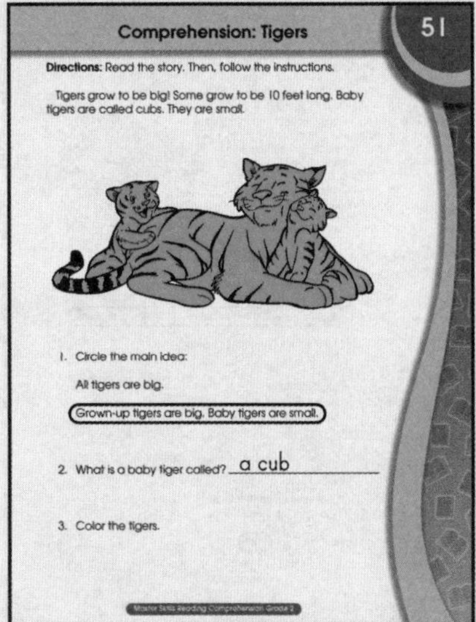

Comprehension: Tigers 51

Directions: Read the story. Then, follow the instructions.

Tigers grow to be big! Some grow to be 10 feet long. Baby tigers are called cubs. They are small.

1. Circle the main idea:

All tigers are big.

Grown-up tigers are big. Baby tigers are small.

2. What is a baby tiger called? a cub

3. Color the tigers.

Master Skills Reading Comprehension Grade 2

51

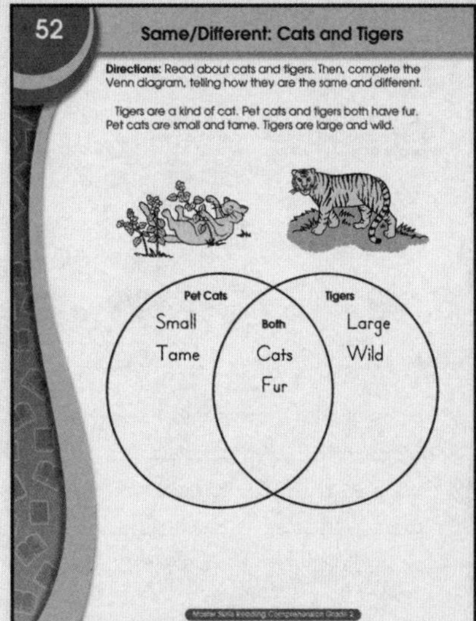

52 Same/Different: Cats and Tigers

Directions: Read about cats and tigers. Then, complete the Venn diagram, telling how they are the same and different.

Tigers are a kind of cat. Pet cats and tigers both have fur. Pet cats are small and tame. Tigers are large and wild.

Master Skills Reading Comprehension Grade 2

52

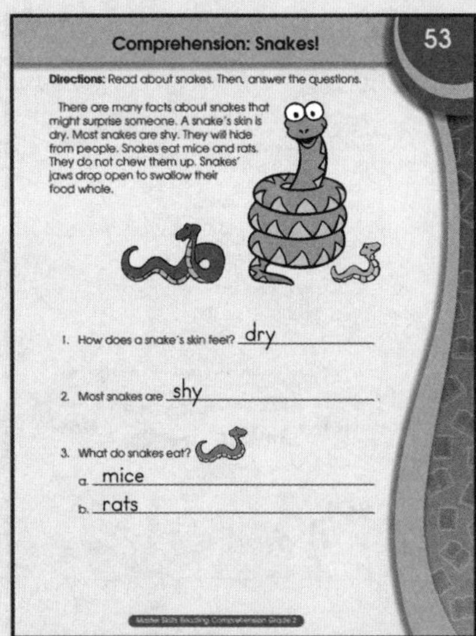

Comprehension: Snakes! 53

Directions: Read about snakes. Then, answer the questions.

There are many facts about snakes that might surprise someone. A snake's skin is dry. Most snakes are shy. They will hide from people. Snakes eat mice and rats. They do not chew them up. Snakes' jaws drop open to swallow their food whole.

1. How does a snake's skin feel? dry

2. Most snakes are shy

3. What do snakes eat?
   a. mice
   b. rats

Master Skills Reading Comprehension Grade 2

53

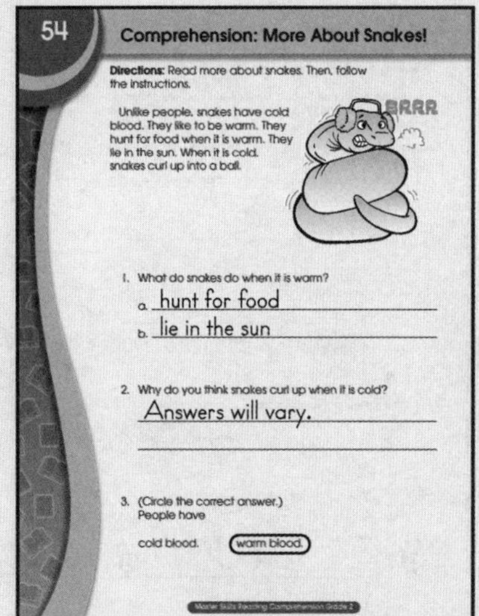

54 Comprehension: More About Snakes!

Directions: Read more about snakes. Then, follow the instructions.

Unlike people, snakes have cold blood. They like to be warm. They hunt for food when it is warm. They lie in the sun. When it is cold, snakes curl up into a ball.

1. What do snakes do when it is warm?
   a. hunt for food
   b. lie in the sun

2. Why do you think snakes curl up when it is cold?
   Answers will vary.

3. (Circle the correct answer.)
   People have

   cold blood. warm blood.

Master Skills Reading Comprehension Grade 2

54

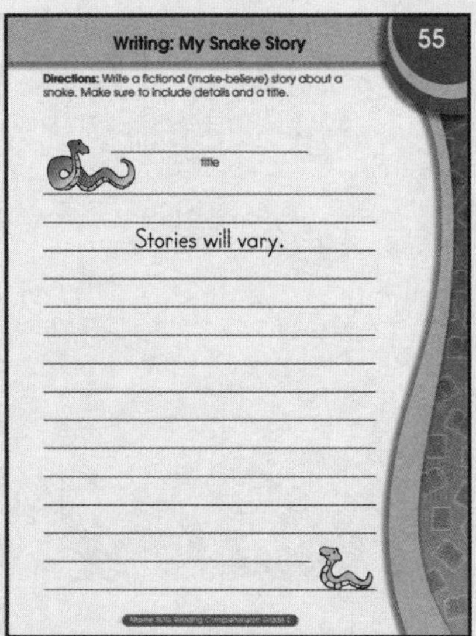

Writing: My Snake Story 55

Directions: Write a fictional (make-believe) story about a snake. Make sure to include details and a title.

title

Stories will vary.

Master Skills Reading Comprehension Grade 2

55

56 Review

Directions: Read about birds. Then, follow the instructions.

Birds use many things to make their nests. They use twigs. They use moss. Birds even use hair and yarn. You can help birds make a nest. First, cut up some yarn. Ask a grown-up to trim your hair. Then, put the yarn and hair outdoors.

1. Circle the main idea:

   Cut your hair to help a bird.

   Birds use many things to make nests.

2. Tell how to help a bird make a nest.
   a. Cut up some yarn.
   b. Trim your hair.
   c. Put the yarn and hair outdoors.

3. Why do you think birds like yarn and hair?
   Answers may include: They are soft, fluffy, easy to carry.

4. Predict what birds will do with the yarn and hair.
   Answers may include: build a nest, line a nest

Master Skills Reading Comprehension Grade 2

56

Answer Key

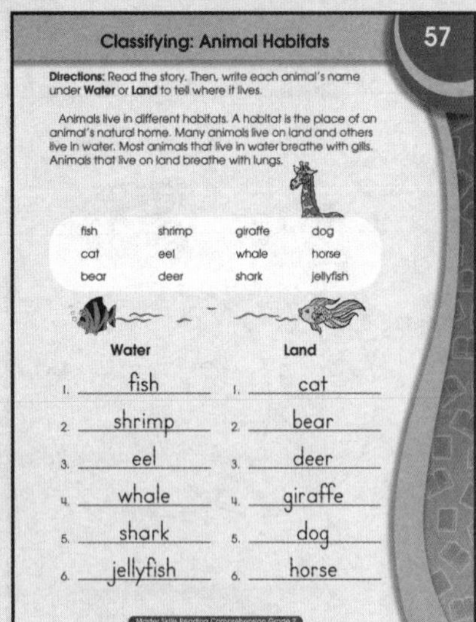

Classifying: Animal Habitats 57

Directions: Read the story. Then, write each animal's name under **Water** or **Land** to tell where it lives.

Animals live in different habitats. A habitat is the place of an animal's natural home. Many animals live on land and others live in water. Most animals that live in water breathe with gills. Animals that live on land breathe with lungs.

fish	shrimp	giraffe	dog
cat	eel	whale	horse
bear	deer	shark	jellyfish

Water	Land
1. fish	1. cat
2. shrimp	2. bear
3. eel	3. deer
4. whale	4. giraffe
5. shark	5. dog
6. jellyfish	6. horse

Master Skills Reading Comprehension Grade 2

57

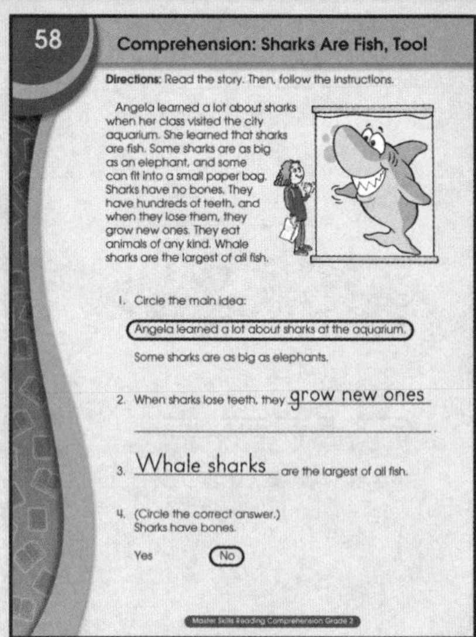

58 Comprehension: Sharks Are Fish, Too!

Directions: Read the story. Then, follow the instructions.

Angela learned a lot about sharks when her class visited the city aquarium. She learned that sharks are fish. Some sharks are as big as an elephant, and some can fit into a small paper bag. Sharks have no bones. They have hundreds of teeth, and when they lose them, they grow new ones. They eat animals of any kind. Whale sharks are the largest of all fish.

1. Circle the main idea:

   (Angela learned a lot about sharks at the aquarium.)

   Some sharks are as big as elephants.

2. When sharks lose teeth, they grow new ones

3. Whale sharks are the largest of all fish.

4. (Circle the correct answer.) Sharks have bones.

   Yes (No)

Master Skills Reading Comprehension Grade 2

58

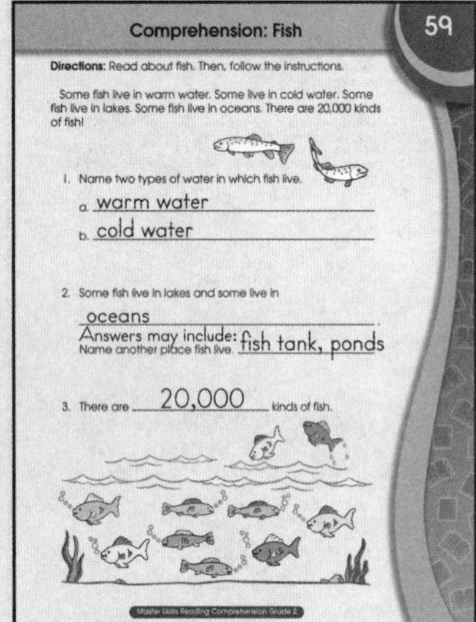

Comprehension: Fish 59

Directions: Read about fish. Then, follow the instructions.

Some fish live in warm water. Some live in cold water. Some fish live in lakes. Some fish live in oceans. There are 20,000 kinds of fish!

1. Name two types of water in which fish live.

   a. warm water

   b. cold water

2. Some fish live in lakes and some live in oceans.

   Name another place fish live. Answers may include: fish tank, ponds

3. There are 20,000 kinds of fish.

Master Skills Reading Comprehension Grade 2

59

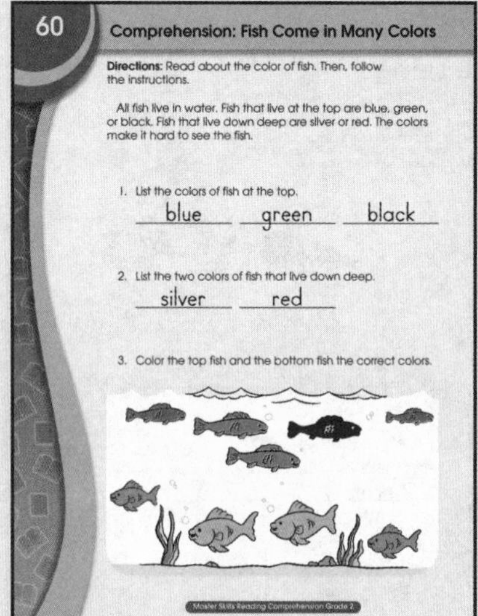

60 Comprehension: Fish Come in Many Colors

Directions: Read about the color of fish. Then, follow the instructions.

All fish live in water. Fish that live at the top are blue, green, or black. Fish that live down deep are silver or red. The colors make it hard to see the fish.

1. List the colors of fish at the top.

   blue green black

2. List the two colors of fish that live down deep.

   silver red

3. Color the top fish and the bottom fish the correct colors.

Master Skills Reading Comprehension Grade 2

60

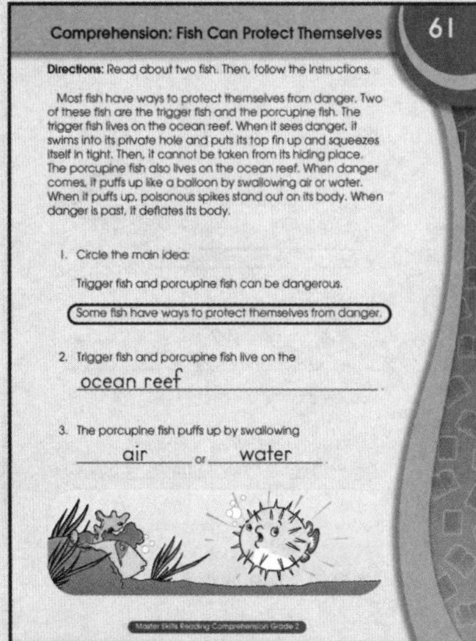

Comprehension: Fish Can Protect Themselves 61

Directions: Read about two fish. Then, follow the instructions.

Most fish have ways to protect themselves from danger. Two of these fish are the trigger fish and the porcupine fish. The trigger fish lives on the ocean reef. When it sees danger, it swims into its private hole and puts its top fin up and squeezes itself in tight. Then, it cannot be taken from its hiding place. The porcupine fish also lives on the ocean reef. When danger comes, it puffs up like a balloon by swallowing air or water. When it puffs up, poisonous spikes stand out on its body. When danger is past, it deflates its body.

1. Circle the main idea:

   Trigger fish and porcupine fish can be dangerous.

   (Some fish have ways to protect themselves from danger.)

2. Trigger fish and porcupine fish live on the ocean reef

3. The porcupine fish puffs up by swallowing air or water.

Master Skills Reading Comprehension Grade 2

61

62 Predicting: Puff and Trigg

Directions: Read about Puff and Trigg. Then, write what happens next in the story.

It was a sunny, warm day in the Pacific Ocean. Puff, the happy porcupine fish, and Trigg, the jolly trigger fish, were having fun playing fish tag. They were good friends. Suddenly, they saw the shadow of a giant fish! It was coming right at them! They knew the giant fish might like eating smaller fish! What did they do?

What did Puff and Trigg do to get away from the giant fish?

Answers will vary.

Master Skills Reading Comprehension Grade 2

62

Answer Key

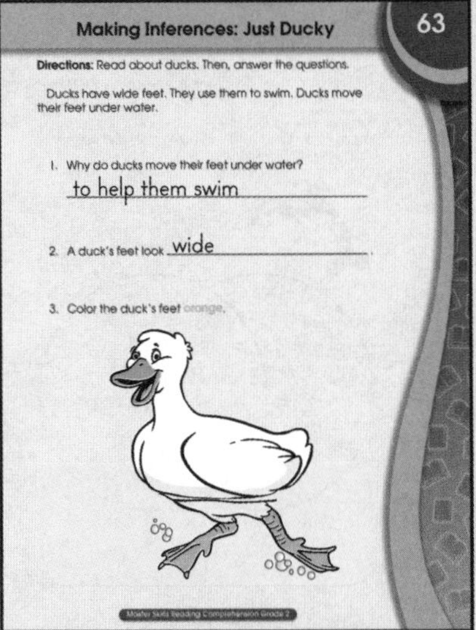

Making Inferences: Just Ducky 63

Directions: Read about ducks. Then, answer the questions.

Ducks have wide feet. They use them to swim. Ducks move their feet under water.

1. Why do ducks move their feet under water?
   to help them swim
2. A duck's feet look wide.
3. Color the duck's feet orange.

Master Skills Reading Comprehension Grade 2

63

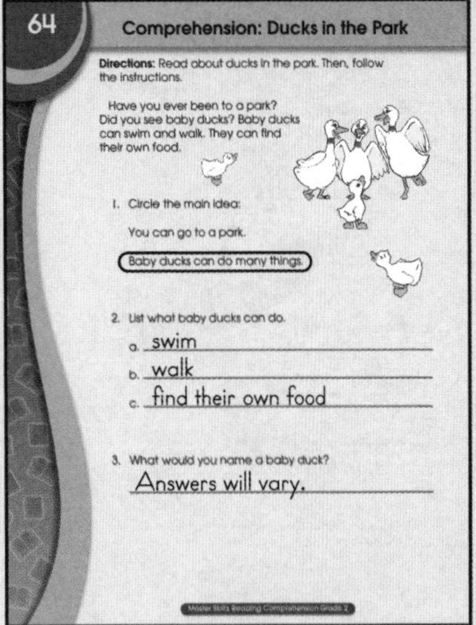

64 Comprehension: Ducks in the Park

Directions: Read about ducks in the park. Then, follow the instructions.

Have you ever been to a park? Did you see baby ducks? Baby ducks can swim and walk. They can find their own food.

1. Circle the main idea:
   You can go to a park.
   (Baby ducks can do many things.)
2. List what baby ducks can do.
   a. swim
   b. walk
   c. find their own food
3. What would you name a baby duck?
   Answers will vary.

Master Skills Reading Comprehension Grade 2

64

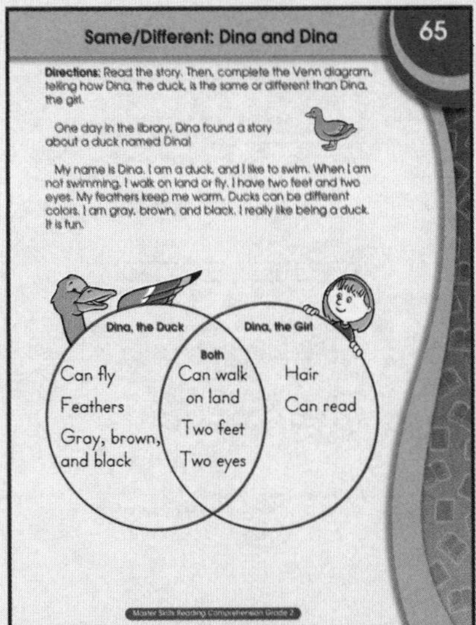

Same/Different: Dina and Dina 65

Directions: Read the story. Then, complete the Venn diagram, telling how Dina, the duck, is the same or different than Dina, the girl.

One day in the library, Dina found a story about a duck named Dina!

My name is Dina. I am a duck, and I like to swim. When I am not swimming, I walk on land or fly. I have two feet and two eyes. My feathers keep me warm. Ducks can be different colors. I am gray, brown, and black. I really like being a duck. It is fun.

Master Skills Reading Comprehension Grade 2

65

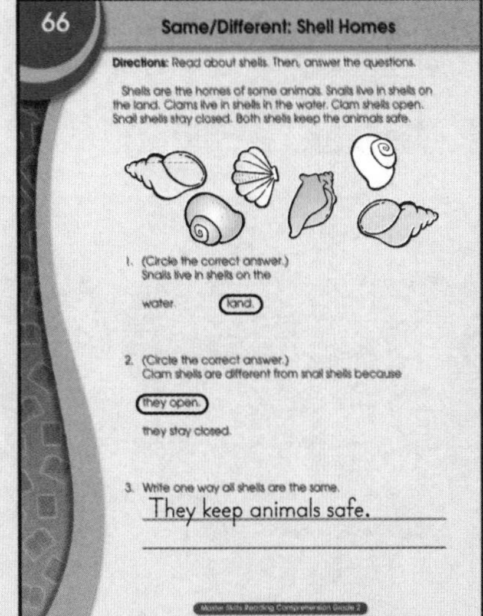

66 Same/Different: Shell Homes

Directions: Read about shells. Then, answer the questions.

Shells are the homes of some animals. Snails live in shells on the land. Clams live in shells in the water. Clam shells open. Snail shells stay closed. Both shells keep the animals safe.

1. (Circle the correct answer.)
   Snails live in shells on the
   water. (land.)
2. (Circle the correct answer.)
   Clam shells are different from snail shells because
   (they open.)
   they stay closed.
3. Write one way all shells are the same.
   They keep animals safe.

Master Skills Reading Comprehension Grade 2

66

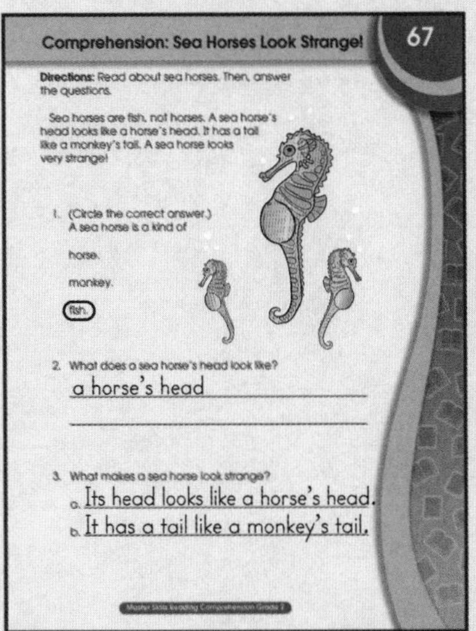

Comprehension: Sea Horses Look Strange! 67

Directions: Read about sea horses. Then, answer the questions.

Sea horses are fish, not horses. A sea horse's head looks like a horse's head. It has a tail like a monkey's tail. A sea horse looks very strange!

1. (Circle the correct answer.)
   A sea horse is a kind of
   horse.
   monkey.
   (fish.)
2. What does a sea horse's head look like?
   a horse's head
3. What makes a sea horse look strange?
   a. Its head looks like a horse's head.
   b. It has a tail like a monkey's tail.

Master Skills Reading Comprehension Grade 2

67

68 Making Inferences: More About Sea Horses

Directions: Read more about sea horses. Then, answer the questions.

A father sea horse helps the mother. He has a small sack, or pouch, on the front of his body. The mother sea horse lays the eggs. She does not keep them. She gives the eggs to the father.

1. What does the mother sea horse do with her eggs?
   She gives them to the father.
2. Where does the father sea horse put the eggs?
   In his pouch.
3. Sea horses can change color. Color the sea horses.

Master Skills Reading Comprehension Grade 2

68

Answer Key

69

Comprehension: Singing Whales

Directions: Read about singing whales. Then, follow the instructions.

Some whales can sing! We cannot understand the words. But we can hear the tune of the humpback whale. Each season, humpback whales sing a different song.

1. Circle the main idea:

All whales can sing.

(Some whales can sing.)

2. Name the kind of whale that sings.

humpback whale

3. How many different songs does the humpback whale sing each year?

1 2 3 (4)

Master Skills Reading Comprehension Grade 2

69

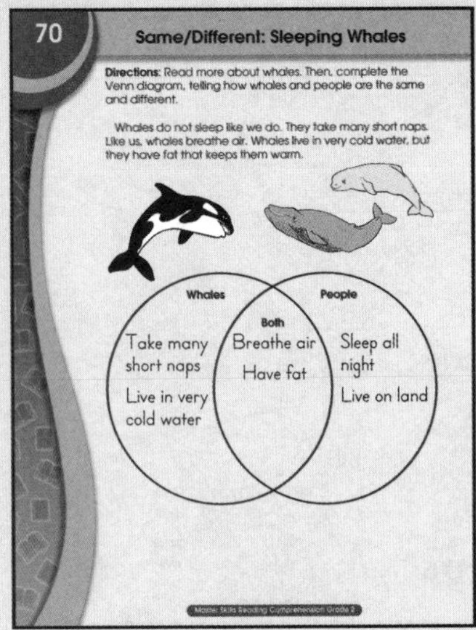

70

Same/Different: Sleeping Whales

Directions: Read more about whales. Then, complete the Venn diagram, telling how whales and people are the same and different.

Whales do not sleep like we do. They take many short naps. Like us, whales breathe air. Whales live in very cold water, but they have fat that keeps them warm.

Whales	Both	People
Take many short naps Live in very cold water	Breathe air Have fat	Sleep all night Live on land

Master Skills Reading Comprehension Grade 2

70

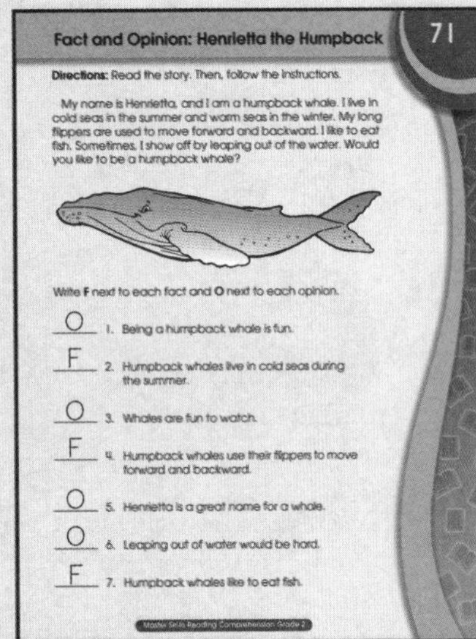

71

Fact and Opinion: Henrietta the Humpback

Directions: Read the story. Then, follow the instructions.

My name is Henrietta, and I am a humpback whale. I live in cold seas in the summer and warm seas in the winter. My long flippers are used to move forward and backward. I like to eat fish. Sometimes, I show off by leaping out of the water. Would you like to be a humpback whale?

Write **F** next to each fact and **O** next to each opinion.

O 1. Being a humpback whale is fun.

F 2. Humpback whales live in cold seas during the summer.

O 3. Whales are fun to watch.

F 4. Humpback whales use their flippers to move forward and backward.

O 5. Henrietta is a great name for a whale.

O 6. Leaping out of water would be hard.

F 7. Humpback whales like to eat fish.

Master Skills Reading Comprehension Grade 2

71

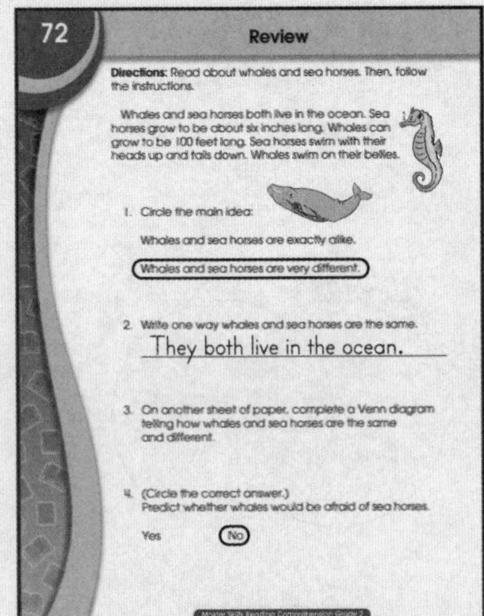

72

Review

Directions: Read about whales and sea horses. Then, follow the instructions.

Whales and sea horses both live in the ocean. Sea horses grow to be about six inches long. Whales can grow to be 100 feet long. Sea horses swim with their heads up and tails down. Whales swim on their bellies.

1. Circle the main idea:

Whales and sea horses are exactly alike.

(Whales and sea horses are very different.)

2. Write one way whales and sea horses are the same.

They both live in the ocean.

3. On another sheet of paper, complete a Venn diagram telling how whales and sea horses are the same and different.

4. (Circle the correct answer.) Predict whether whales would be afraid of sea horses.

Yes (No)

Master Skills Reading Comprehension Grade 2

72

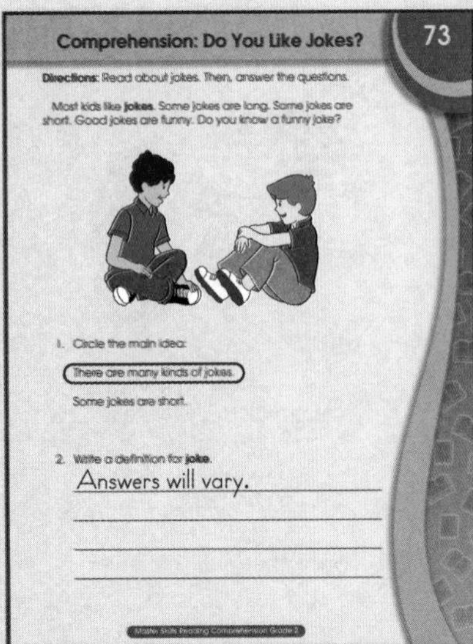

73

Comprehension: Do You Like Jokes?

Directions: Read about jokes. Then, answer the questions.

Most kids like **jokes**. Some jokes are long. Some jokes are short. Good jokes are funny. Do you know a funny joke?

1. Circle the main idea:

(There are many kinds of jokes.)

Some jokes are short.

2. Write a definition for **joke**.

Answers will vary.

Master Skills Reading Comprehension Grade 2

73

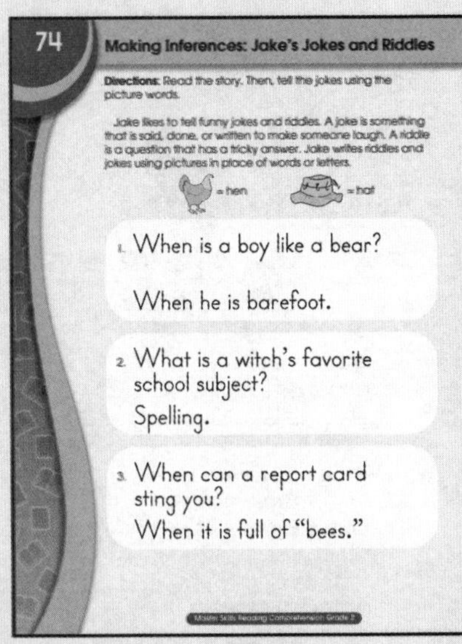

74

Making Inferences: Jake's Jokes and Riddles

Directions: Read the story. Then, tell the jokes using the picture words.

Jake likes to tell funny jokes and riddles. A joke is something that is said, done, or written to make someone laugh. A riddle is a question that has a tricky answer. Jake writes riddles and jokes using pictures in place of words or letters.

= hen = hat

1. When is a boy like a bear?

When he is barefoot.

2. What is a witch's favorite school subject?

Spelling.

3. When can a report card sting you?

When it is full of "bees."

Master Skills Reading Comprehension Grade 2

74

Answer Key

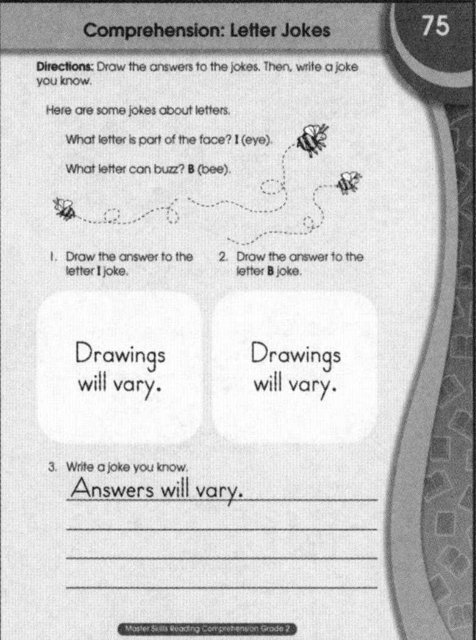

75

Comprehension: Letter Jokes

Directions: Draw the answers to the jokes. Then, write a joke you know.

Here are some jokes about letters.

What letter is part of the face? **I** (eye).

What letter can buzz? **B** (bee).

1. Draw the answer to the letter **I** joke.
2. Draw the answer to the letter **B** joke.

Drawings will vary.

Drawings will vary.

3. Write a joke you know.

Answers will vary.

Master Skills Reading Comprehension Grade 2

75

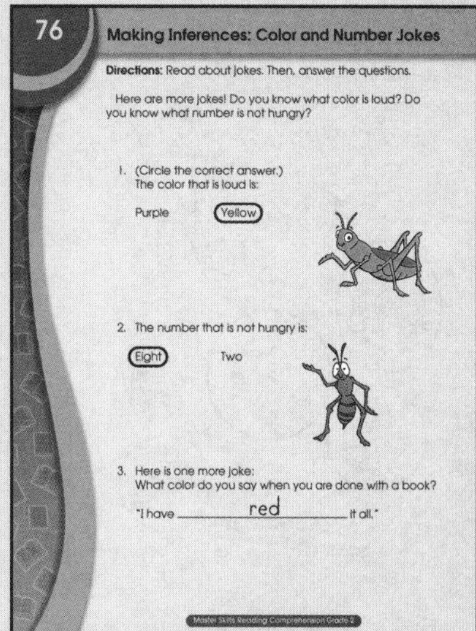

76

Making Inferences: Color and Number Jokes

Directions: Read about jokes. Then, answer the questions.

Here are more jokes! Do you know what color is loud? Do you know what number is not hungry?

1. (Circle the correct answer.) The color that is loud is:

Purple (Yellow)

2. The number that is not hungry is:

(Eight) Two

3. Here is one more joke: What color do you say when you are done with a book?

"I have red it all."

Master Skills Reading Comprehension Grade 2

76

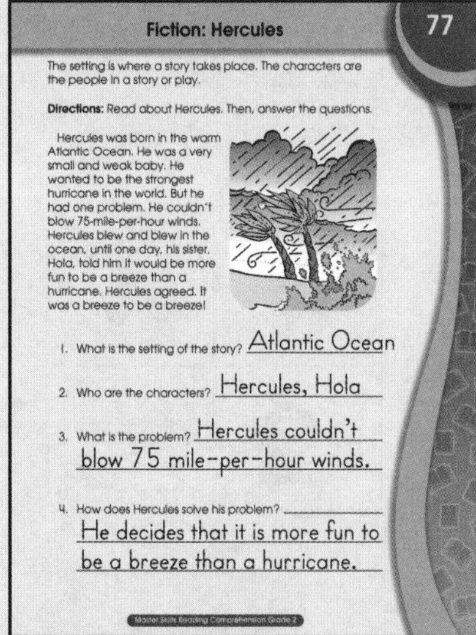

Fiction: Hercules

77

The setting is where a story takes place. The characters are the people in a story or play.

Directions: Read about Hercules. Then, answer the questions.

Hercules was born in the warm Atlantic Ocean. He was a very small and weak baby. He wanted to be the strongest hurricane in the world. But he had one problem. He couldn't blow 75-mile-per-hour winds. Hercules blew and blew in the ocean, until one day, his sister, Hola, told him it would be more fun to be a breeze than a hurricane. Hercules agreed. It was a breeze to be a breeze!

1. What is the setting of the story? Atlantic Ocean
2. Who are the characters? Hercules, Hola
3. What is the problem? Hercules couldn't blow 75 mile-per-hour winds.
4. How does Hercules solve his problem? He decides that it is more fun to be a breeze than a hurricane.

Master Skills Reading Comprehension Grade 2

77

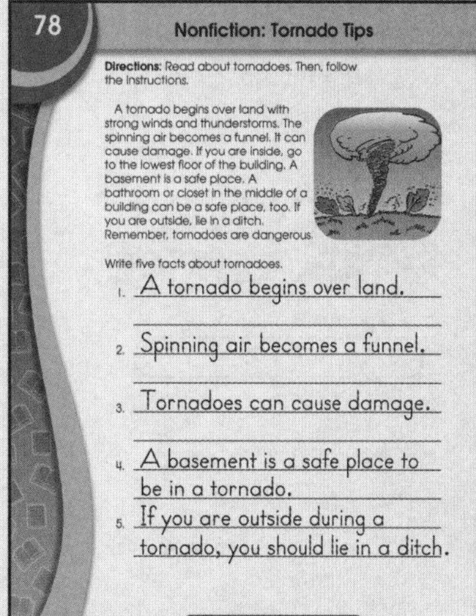

78

Nonfiction: Tornado Tips

Directions: Read about tornadoes. Then, follow the instructions.

A tornado begins over land with strong winds and thunderstorms. The spinning air becomes a funnel. It can cause damage. If you are inside, go to the lowest floor of the building. A basement is a safe place. A bathroom or closet in the middle of a building can be a safe place, too. If you are outside, lie in a ditch. Remember, tornadoes are dangerous.

Write five facts about tornadoes.

1. A tornado begins over land.
2. Spinning air becomes a funnel.
3. Tornadoes can cause damage.
4. A basement is a safe place to be in a tornado.
5. If you are outside during a tornado, you should lie in a ditch.

Master Skills Reading Comprehension Grade 2

78

Comprehension: A Winter Story

79

Directions: Read about winter. Then, follow the instructions.

It is cold in winter. Snow falls. Water freezes. Most kids like to play outdoors. Some kids make a snowman. Some kids skate. What do you do in winter?

1. Circle the main idea:

Snow falls in winter.

(In winter, there are many things to do outside.)

2. Write two things about winter weather.

1) Answers will vary.

2)

3. Write what you like to do in winter.

Answers will vary.

Master Skills Reading Comprehension Grade 2

79

80

Sequencing: Making a Snowman

Directions: Read about how to make a snowman. Then, follow the instructions.

It is fun to make a snowman. First, find things for the snowman's eyes and nose. Dress warmly. Then, go outdoors. Roll a big snowball. Then, roll another to put on top of it. Now, roll a small snowball for the head. Put on the snowman's face.

1 2 3 4

1. Number the pictures in order.
2. Write two things to do before going outdoors.

1) Dress warmly.

2) Find things for the snowman's eyes and nose.

Master Skills Reading Comprehension Grade 2

80

Answer Key

81

Classifying: A Rainy Day

Directions: Read the story. Then, circle the objects Jonathan needs to stay dry.

It is raining. Jonathan wants to play outdoors. What should he wear to stay dry? What should he carry to stay dry?

Master Skills Reading Comprehension Grade 2

81

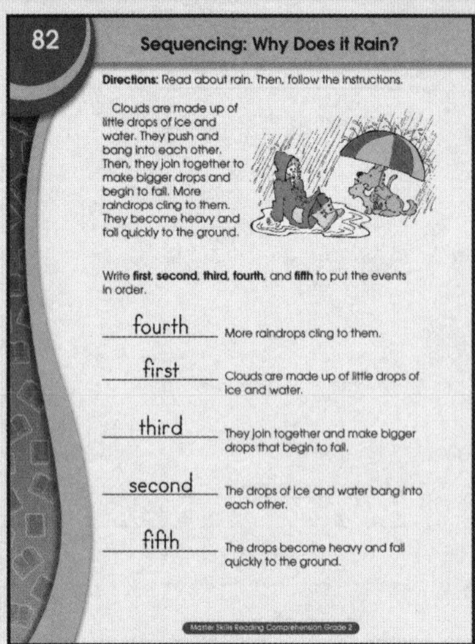

82

Sequencing: Why Does it Rain?

Directions: Read about rain. Then, follow the instructions.

Clouds are made up of little drops of ice and water. They push and bang into each other. Then, they join together to make bigger drops and begin to fall. More raindrops cling to them. They become heavy and fall quickly to the ground.

Write **first**, **second**, **third**, **fourth**, and **fifth** to put the events in order.

fourth — More raindrops cling to them.

first — Clouds are made up of little drops of ice and water.

third — They join together and make bigger drops that begin to fall.

second — The drops of ice and water bang into each other.

fifth — The drops become heavy and fall quickly to the ground.

Master Skills Reading Comprehension Grade 2

82

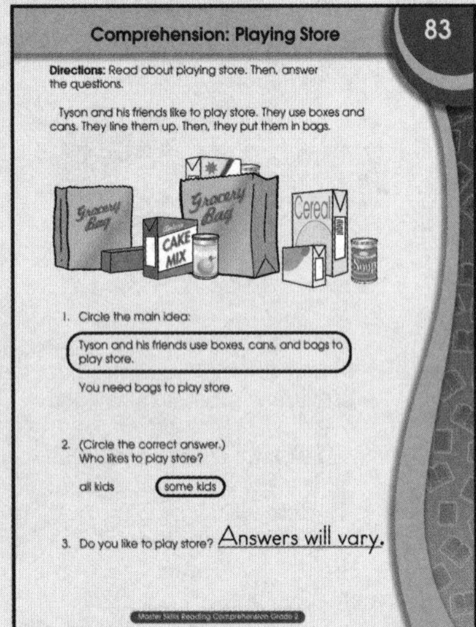

83

Comprehension: Playing Store

Directions: Read about playing store. Then, answer the questions.

Tyson and his friends like to play store. They use boxes and cans. They line them up. Then, they put them in bags.

1. Circle the main idea:

   (Tyson and his friends use boxes, cans, and bags to play store.)

   You need bags to play store.

2. (Circle the correct answer.) Who likes to play store?

   all kids (some kids)

3. Do you like to play store? Answers will vary.

Master Skills Reading Comprehension Grade 2

83

84

Sequencing: Packing Bags

Directions: Read about packing bags. Then, number the objects in the order they should be packed.

Cans are heavy. Put them in first. Then, put in boxes. Now, put in the apple. Put the bread in last.

3 (apple)	1 (soup cans)
2 (cereal)	4 (bread)

Master Skills Reading Comprehension Grade 2

84

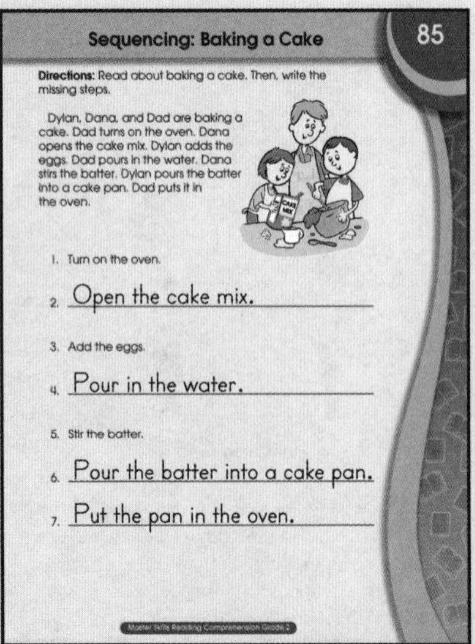

85

Sequencing: Baking a Cake

Directions: Read about baking a cake. Then, write the missing steps.

Dylan, Dana, and Dad are baking a cake. Dad turns on the oven. Dana opens the cake mix. Dylan adds the eggs. Dad pours in the water. Dana stirs the batter. Dylan pours the batter into a cake pan. Dad puts it in the oven.

1. Turn on the oven.
2. Open the cake mix.
3. Add the eggs.
4. Pour in the water.
5. Stir the batter.
6. Pour the batter into a cake pan.
7. Put the pan in the oven.

Master Skills Reading Comprehension Grade 2

85

86

Making Deductions: A Menu

Directions: Look at the clues below. Fill in the menu.

Sunday	chef salad
Monday	stew
Tuesday	chicken
Wednesday	corn-on-the-cob
Thursday	potpie
Friday	pizza
Saturday	fish

1. Mom fixed stew on Monday.
2. Dad fixed chef salad the day before that.
3. Lila made a potpie three days after Mom fixed stew.
4. Ross fixed corn-on-the-cob the day before Lila made potpie.
5. Mom fixed pizza the day after Lila made the potpie.
6. Lila cooked fish the day before Dad fixed chef salad.
7. Dad is making chicken today. What day is it?

   Tuesday

Master Skills Reading Comprehension Grade 2

86

Answer Key

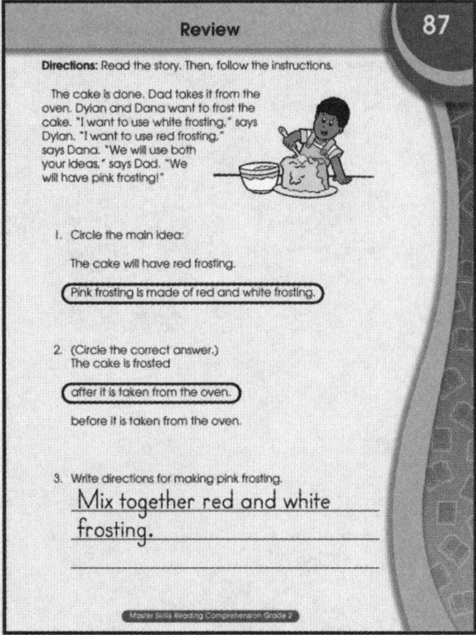

Review

87

Directions: Read the story. Then, follow the instructions.

The cake is done. Dad takes it from the oven. Dylan and Dana want to frost the cake. "I want to use white frosting," says Dylan. "I want to use red frosting," says Dana. "We will use both your ideas," says Dad. "We will have pink frosting!"

1. Circle the main idea:

   The cake will have red frosting.

   Pink frosting is made of red and white frosting.

2. (Circle the correct answer.) The cake is frosted

   after it is taken from the oven.

   before it is taken from the oven.

3. Write directions for making pink frosting.

   Mix together red and white frosting.

Master Skills Reading Comprehension Grade 2

87

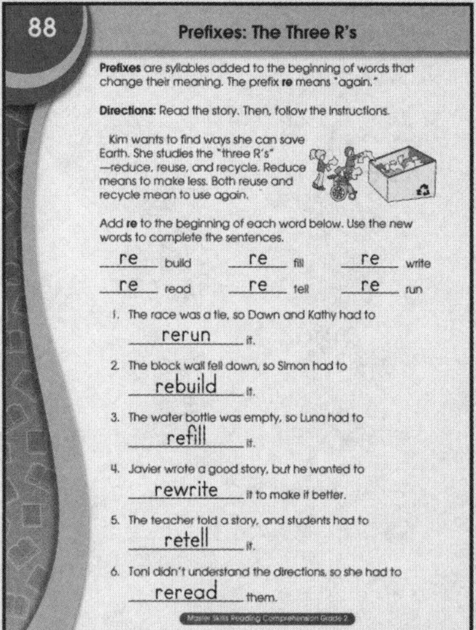

Prefixes: The Three R's

88

Prefixes are syllables added to the beginning of words that change their meaning. The prefix **re** means "again."

Directions: Read the story. Then, follow the instructions.

Kim wants to find ways she can save Earth. She studies the "three R's" —reduce, reuse, and recycle. Reduce means to make less. Both reuse and recycle mean to use again.

Add **re** to the beginning of each word below. Use the new words to complete the sentences.

re build   re fill   re write

re read   re tell   re run

1. The race was a tie, so Dawn and Kathy had to rerun it.
2. The block wall fell down, so Simon had to rebuild it.
3. The water bottle was empty, so Luna had to refill it.
4. Javier wrote a good story, but he wanted to rewrite it to make it better.
5. The teacher told a story, and students had to retell it.
6. Toni didn't understand the directions, so she had to reread them.

Master Skills Reading Comprehension Grade 2

88

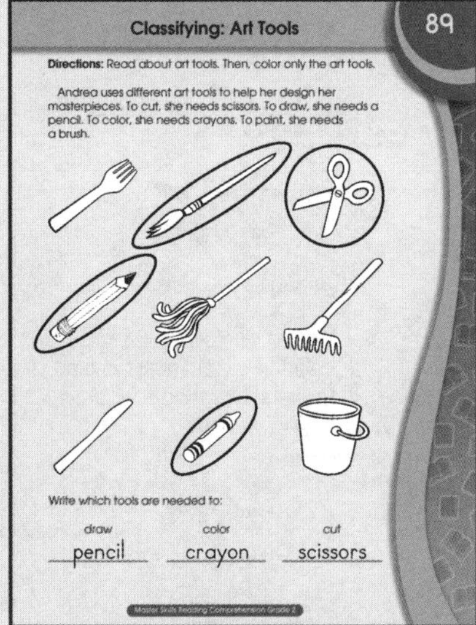

Classifying: Art Tools

89

Directions: Read about art tools. Then, color only the art tools.

Andrea uses different art tools to help her design her masterpieces. To cut, she needs scissors. To draw, she needs a pencil. To color, she needs crayons. To paint, she needs a brush.

Write which tools are needed to:

draw	color	cut
pencil	crayon	scissors

Master Skills Reading Comprehension Grade 2

89

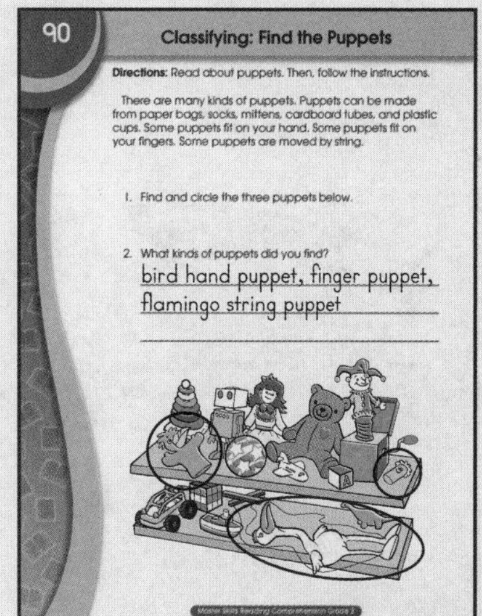

Classifying: Find the Puppets

90

Directions: Read about puppets. Then, follow the instructions.

There are many kinds of puppets. Puppets can be made from paper bags, socks, mittens, cardboard tubes, and plastic cups. Some puppets fit on your hand. Some puppets fit on your fingers. Some puppets are moved by string.

1. Find and circle the three puppets below.
2. What kinds of puppets did you find?

   bird hand puppet, finger puppet, flamingo string puppet

Master Skills Reading Comprehension Grade 2

90

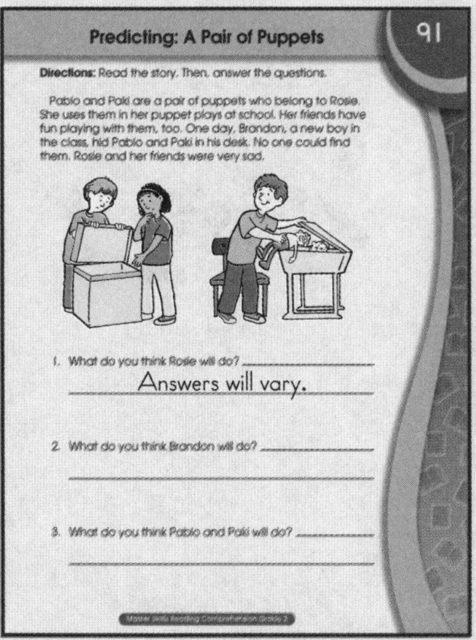

Predicting: A Pair of Puppets

91

Directions: Read the story. Then, answer the questions.

Pablo and Paki are a pair of puppets who belong to Rosie. She uses them in her puppet plays at school. Her friends have fun playing with them, too. One day, Brandon, a new boy in the class, hid Pablo and Paki in his desk. No one could find them. Rosie and her friends were very sad.

1. What do you think Rosie will do?

   Answers will vary.

2. What do you think Brandon will do?
3. What do you think Pablo and Paki will do?

Master Skills Reading Comprehension Grade 2

91

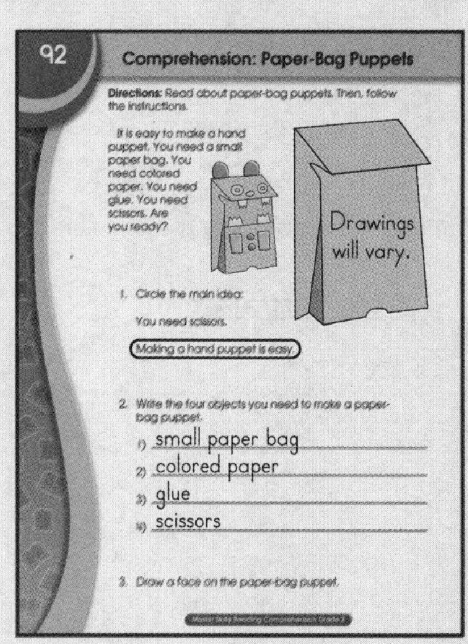

Comprehension: Paper-Bag Puppets

92

Directions: Read about paper-bag puppets. Then, follow the instructions.

It is easy to make a hand puppet. You need a small paper bag. You need colored paper. You need glue. You need scissors. Are you ready?

Drawings will vary.

1. Circle the main idea:

   You need scissors.

   Making a hand puppet is easy.

2. Write the four objects you need to make a paper-bag puppet.

   1) small paper bag
   2) colored paper
   3) glue
   4) scissors

3. Draw a face on the paper-bag puppet.

Master Skills Reading Comprehension Grade 2

92

Answer Key

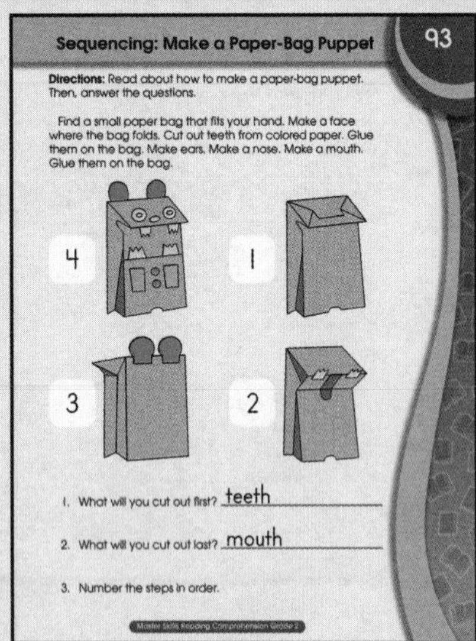

Sequencing: Make a Paper-Bag Puppet

93

Directions: Read about how to make a paper-bag puppet. Then, answer the questions.

Find a small paper bag that fits your hand. Make a face where the bag folds. Cut out teeth from colored paper. Glue them on the bag. Make ears. Make a nose. Make a mouth. Glue them on the bag.

4 1 3 2

1. What will you cut out first? teeth
2. What will you cut out last? mouth
3. Number the steps in order.

Master Skills Reading Comprehension Grade 2

93

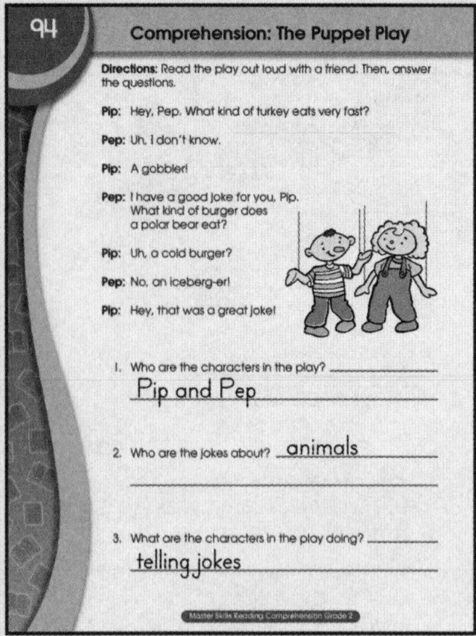

Comprehension: The Puppet Play

94

Directions: Read the play out loud with a friend. Then, answer the questions.

Pip: Hey, Pep. What kind of turkey eats very fast?

Pep: Uh, I don't know.

Pip: A gobbler!

Pep: I have a good joke for you, Pip. What kind of burger does a polar bear eat?

Pip: Uh, a cold burger?

Pep: No, an iceberg-er!

Pip: Hey, that was a great joke!

1. Who are the characters in the play? Pip and Pep
2. Who are the jokes about? animals
3. What are the characters in the play doing? telling jokes

Master Skills Reading Comprehension Grade 2

94

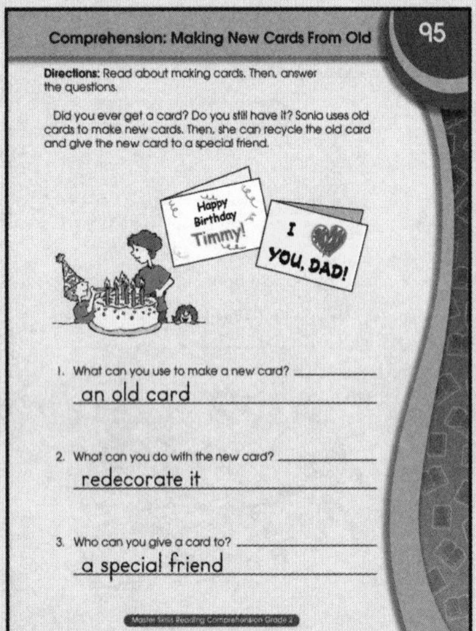

Comprehension: Making New Cards From Old

95

Directions: Read about making cards. Then, answer the questions.

Did you ever get a card? Do you still have it? Sonia uses old cards to make new cards. Then, she can recycle the old card and give the new card to a special friend.

1. What can you use to make a new card? an old card
2. What can you do with the new card? redecorate it
3. Who can you give a card to? a special friend

Master Skills Reading Comprehension Grade 2

95

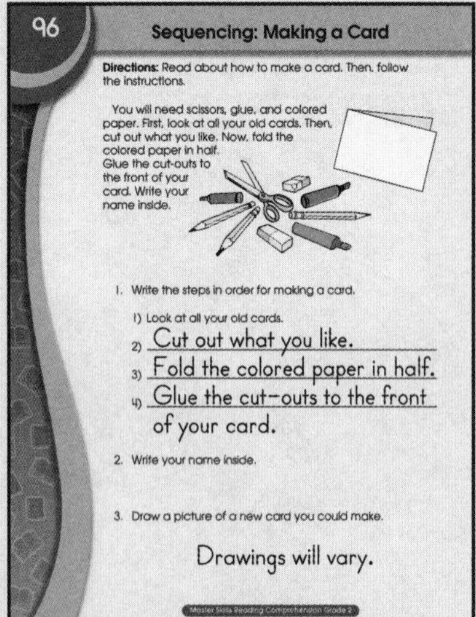

Sequencing: Making a Card

96

Directions: Read about how to make a card. Then, follow the instructions.

You will need scissors, glue, and colored paper. First, look at all your old cards. Then, cut out what you like. Now, fold the colored paper in half. Glue the cut-outs to the front of your card. Write your name inside.

1. Write the steps in order for making a card.
   1) Look at all your old cards.
   2) Cut out what you like.
   3) Fold the colored paper in half.
   4) Glue the cut-outs to the front of your card.
2. Write your name inside.
3. Draw a picture of a new card you could make.

Drawings will vary.

Master Skills Reading Comprehension Grade 2

96

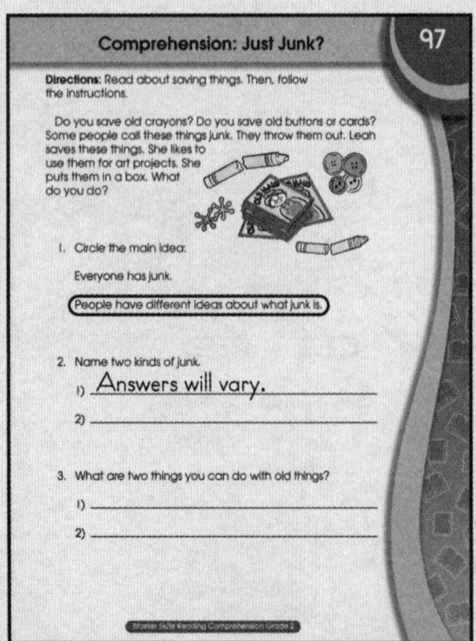

Comprehension: Just Junk?

97

Directions: Read about saving things. Then, follow the instructions.

Do you save old crayons? Do you save old buttons or cards? Some people call these things junk. They throw them out. Leah saves these things. She likes to use them for art projects. She puts them in a box. What do you do?

1. Circle the main idea:

   Everyone has junk.

   (People have different ideas about what junk is.)
2. Name two kinds of junk.
   1) Answers will vary.
   2)
3. What are two things you can do with old things?
   1)
   2)

Master Skills Reading Comprehension Grade 2

97

Following Directions: Color the Junk

98

Directions: Color the buttons red. Color the jacks silver. Color the crayons green. Then, draw and color some of the things you save.

Answers will vary.

Master Skills Reading Comprehension Grade 2

98

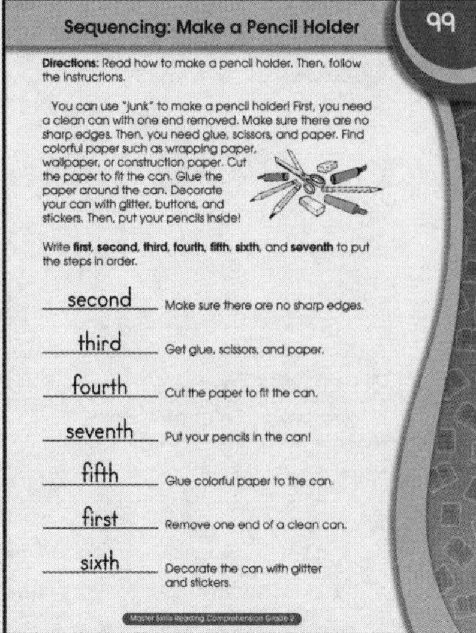

Sequencing: Make a Pencil Holder 99

Directions: Read how to make a pencil holder. Then, follow the instructions.

You can use "junk" to make a pencil holder! First, you need a clean can with one end removed. Make sure there are no sharp edges. Then, you need glue, scissors, and paper. Find colorful paper such as wrapping paper, wallpaper, or construction paper. Cut the paper to fit the can. Glue the paper around the can. Decorate your can with glitter, buttons, and stickers. Then, put your pencils inside!

Write **first**, **second**, **third**, **fourth**, **fifth**, **sixth**, and **seventh** to put the steps in order.

second Make sure there are no sharp edges.

third Get glue, scissors, and paper.

fourth Cut the paper to fit the can.

seventh Put your pencils in the can!

fifth Glue colorful paper to the can.

first Remove one end of a clean can.

sixth Decorate the can with glitter and stickers.

Master Skills Reading Comprehension Grade 2

99

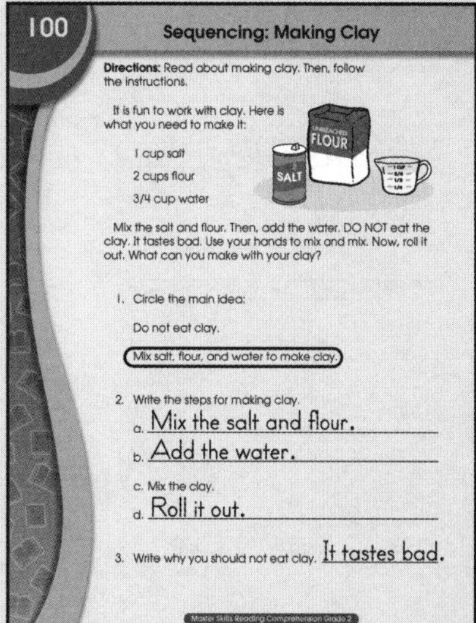

100 Sequencing: Making Clay

Directions: Read about making clay. Then, follow the instructions.

It is fun to work with clay. Here is what you need to make it:

1 cup salt

2 cups flour

3/4 cup water

Mix the salt and flour. Then, add the water. DO NOT eat the clay. It tastes bad. Use your hands to mix and mix. Now, roll it out. What can you make with your clay?

1. Circle the main idea:

   Do not eat clay.

   (Mix salt, flour, and water to make clay.)

2. Write the steps for making clay.

   a. Mix the salt and flour.

   b. Add the water.

   c. Mix the clay.

   d. Roll it out.

3. Write why you should not eat clay. It tastes bad.

Master Skills Reading Comprehension Grade 2

100

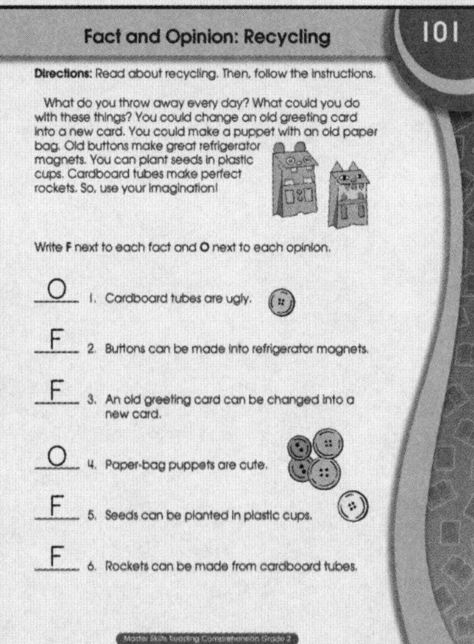

Fact and Opinion: Recycling 101

Directions: Read about recycling. Then, follow the instructions.

What do you throw away every day? What could you do with these things? You could change an old greeting card into a new card. You could make a puppet with an old paper bag. Old buttons make great refrigerator magnets. You can plant seeds in plastic cups. Cardboard tubes make perfect rockets. So, use your imagination!

Write **F** next to each fact and **O** next to each opinion.

O 1. Cardboard tubes are ugly.

F 2. Buttons can be made into refrigerator magnets.

F 3. An old greeting card can be changed into a new card.

O 4. Paper-bag puppets are cute.

F 5. Seeds can be planted in plastic cups.

F 6. Rockets can be made from cardboard tubes.

Master Skills Reading Comprehension Grade 2

101

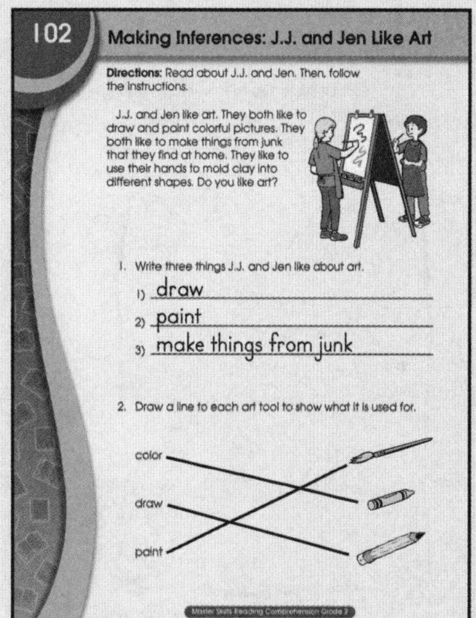

102 Making Inferences: J.J. and Jen Like Art

Directions: Read about J.J. and Jen. Then, follow the instructions.

J.J. and Jen like art. They both like to draw and paint colorful pictures. They both like to make things from junk that they find at home. They like to use their hands to mold clay into different shapes. Do you like art?

1. Write three things J.J. and Jen like about art.

   1) draw

   2) paint

   3) make things from junk

2. Draw a line to each art tool to show what it is used for.

   color

   draw

   paint

Master Skills Reading Comprehension Grade 2

102

Fiction and Nonfiction: Which Is It? 103

Directions: Read about fiction and nonfiction books. Then, follow the instructions.

There are many kinds of books. Some books have make-believe stories about princesses and dragons. Some books contain poetry and rhymes, like Mother Goose. These are fiction. Some books contain facts about space and plants. And still, other books have stories about famous people in history, like Abraham Lincoln. These are nonfiction.

Write **F** for fiction and **NF** for nonfiction.

F 1. nursery rhyme

F 2. fairy tale

NF 3. true life story of a famous athlete

F 4. Aesop's fables

NF 5. dictionary entry about foxes

NF 6. weather report

F 7. story about a talking tree

NF 8. story about animal habitats

F 9. riddles and jokes

Master Skills Reading Comprehension Grade 2

103

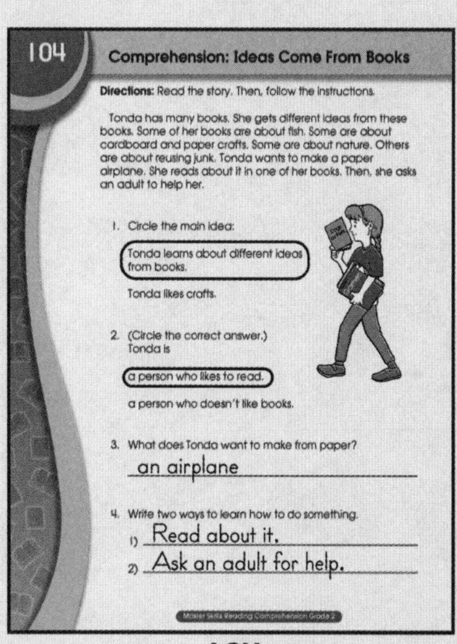

104 Comprehension: Ideas Come From Books

Directions: Read the story. Then, follow the instructions.

Tonda has many books. She gets different ideas from these books. Some of her books are about fish. Some are about cardboard and paper crafts. Some are about nature. Others are about reusing junk. Tonda wants to make a paper airplane. She reads about it in one of her books. Then, she asks an adult to help her.

1. Circle the main idea:

   (Tonda learns about different ideas from books.)

   Tonda likes crafts.

2. (Circle the correct answer.) Tonda is

   (a person who likes to read.)

   a person who doesn't like books.

3. What does Tonda want to make from paper?

   an airplane

4. Write two ways to learn how to do something.

   1) Read about it.

   2) Ask an adult for help.

Master Skills Reading Comprehension Grade 2

104

Answer Key

Review 105

Directions: Read the story. Then, answer the questions.

Randa, Emily, Ali, Dave, Liesl, and Deana all love to read. Every Tuesday, they all go to the library together and pick out their favorite books. Randa likes books about fish. Emily likes books about sports and athletes. Ali likes books about art. Dave likes books about wild animals. Liesl likes books with riddles and puzzles. Deanna likes books about cats and dogs.

1. Circle the main idea:

   Randa, Emily, Ali, Dave, Liesl, and Deana are good friends.

   Randa, Emily, Ali, Dave, Liesl, and Deana all like books.

2. Who do you think might grow up to be an artist?

   Ali

3. Who do you think might grow up to be an oceanographer (someone who studies the ocean)?

   Randa

4. Who do you think might grow up to be a veterinarian (an animal doctor)?

   Deanna

Master Skills Reading Comprehension Grade 2

105

106 All About You!

In this book you learned about many children and what they like to do. You have many interests, too!

Directions: Write a story telling what you like to do. Then, draw a picture to go with your story on the next page.

Stories will vary.

Master Skills Reading Comprehension Grade 2

106

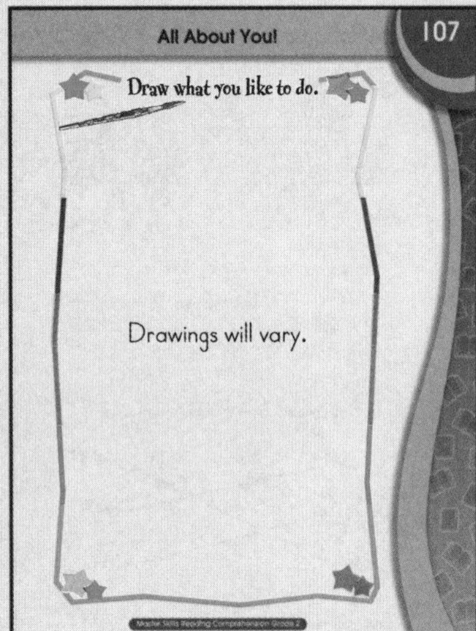

All About You! 107

Draw what you like to do.

Drawings will vary.

Master Skills Reading Comprehension Grade 2

107

Predicting

Before reading a book with your child, ask him or her questions about the story and scan the illustrations. Ask questions beginning with **who**, **what**, **why**, **when**, and **how**. For example: What do you think this book is about? What do you think the title means? Who is this on the cover of the book? What is he or she doing? Do you think this is a true story or a make-believe story?

Recalling Details

Have your child choose a character from a story and write or tell about the character. Ask him or her to draw a picture of the character.

Read a fairy tale with your child. Ask him or her to tell or write the story from a different point of view. For example: Make the troll the good character in *Three Billy Goats Gruff* and the goats the bad characters.

Have your child make a story chart for a book, displaying the important events that happened at the beginning, middle, and end of the story.

Your child can create a shoebox diorama displaying a scene from a favorite story, book, play, poem, and so on. A diorama is a 3-D scene that includes characters and objects from a story, displayed in an open box, similar to a stage. Encourage your child to be creative!

Shoebox Diorama

Following Directions

Have your child read and follow directions for constructing a model, playing a game, preparing a recipe, and so on. Ask your child to write his or her own directions for making a simple recipe or playing a simple game.

Sequencing

Invite your child to recreate a story as a comic strip. List six or more important events or scenes from a story in sequence. Then, have your child write each event on a separate sheet of paper and draw an accompanying picture. Glue the pages in order on large sheets of colorful construction paper. For a sequencing activity, invite your child to put the story events in order before gluing them down.

Cut apart comic strips in newspapers for your child. Have your child read the dialogue, examine the pictures, and then put the whole comic strip back together in order.